Taylor Swift
In Her Own Words

Taylor Swift
In Her Own Words
Young Reader Edition

EDITED BY
Helena Hunt

A B2 BOOK

AGATE

CHICAGO

ISBN-13: 978-1-57284-338-7
ISBN-10: 1-57284-338-1
eISBN-13: 978-1-57284-886-3
eISBN-10: 1-57284-886-3

Printed in the United States of America

The Library of Congress has cataloged the earlier edition of this book as follows:

Names: Swift, Taylor, 1989- | Hunt, Helena, editor.
Title: Taylor Swift : in her own words / edited by Helena Hunt.
Description: Chicago : B2 Books, [2019]
Identifiers: LCCN 2019019795 (print) | LCCN 2019021216 (ebook) | ISBN
  9781572842786 (pbk. : alk. paper) | ISBN 1572842784 (pbk. : alk. paper) |
  ISBN 9781572848351 (ebook) | ISBN 1572848359 (ebook)
Subjects: LCSH: Swift, Taylor, 1989---Quotations. | Singers--United
  States--Quotations. | Country musicians--United States--Quotations.
Classification: LCC ML420.S968 A5 2019 (ebook) | LCC ML420.S968
(print) | DDC
  782.421642092--dc23
LC record available at https://lccn.loc.gov/2019021216

10 9 8 7 6 5 4 3 2 1   24 25 26 27 28

B2 Books is an imprint of Agate Publishing. Agate books are available in bulk at discount prices. For more information, go to agatepublishing.com.

I feel no need to burn down the house I built by hand. I can make additions to it. I can redecorate. But I built this. And so I'm not going to sit there and say, "Oh, I wish I hadn't had corkscrew-curly hair and worn cowboy boots and sundresses to awards shows when I was 17; I wish I hadn't gone through that fairy-tale phase where I just wanted to wear princess dresses to awards shows every single time." Because I made those choices. I did that. It was part of me growing up. It wasn't some committee going, "You know what Taylor needs to be this year?"

—Taylor Swift

Contents

Introduction

Since she was eleven or twelve years old and first learned to play guitar on her parents' Christmas tree farm in Pennsylvania, Taylor Swift has been an image maker and a storyteller.

Swift has said that she always knew she needed to be different from other kids who dreamed of stardom. She had to work harder and be better. She learned the guitar, performed at barbecues and Boy Scout events, and delivered demos to Nashville music executives when she was still in junior high. But her self-written songs—which even from a young age are catchy and relatable—were what really set her apart.

In Nashville (where Swift convinced her parents to move when she was fourteen), most labels argued that country music fans weren't interested in the songs about bullying, high school romance, and rejection that she wrote between classes. But Swift knew more about her image and its appeal than they did. After scouting her in Nashville, Scott Borchetta offered to sign Swift to his yet-to-be-created label, Big Machine Records. Swift committed, pairing up with the label that would put out her first six albums.

And Swift very quickly did find the audience that was waiting for her. Her first single, "Tim McGraw," and her self-titled album, *Taylor Swift*, both made it onto the country charts and got attention from awards shows and a growing fan base. Swift worked tirelessly to promote the music, homeschooling to keep up with her tour and recording schedules. In interviews with radio DJs and TV hosts she comes off as a normal teen girl—in awe of her success, quick to laugh at a joke, eager to gossip about boyfriends and junior high bullies. By showing that the experiences of teen girls are natural, interesting, and worth singing about, she turned her normalcy into an abnormal level of success.

By the time *Fearless* and *Speak Now* were released, Swift's success was beyond question. *Fearless*, only her second album, peaked at number one on the Billboard 200 chart, won her the Grammy for Album of the Year, and launched her on her first global headlining tour. On *Speak Now*, the subjects—bullying and heartbreak—are the same as they were on *Taylor Swift* but go way beyond high school. Her love interests on *Speak Now* are no longer the captain of the football team or the boy next door: they are (reportedly—she has rarely discussed her love life with the media) John Mayer, Joe Jonas, and Taylor Lautner, all celebrities in their own right. The music gets much bigger too, her simple country melodies transitioning into sweeping pop choruses.

Her next album would be *Red*, a major step away from her old country sound and toward both pop and a set of more adult concerns. *Red* was the first album Swift wrote in her twenties, and the songs, which largely dwell on heartbreak (reportedly from her relationship with Jake Gyllenhaal), show the growth she had experienced since becoming a teen star and a willingness to experiment with new sounds. But even though *Red* repackages her heartbreak, the emotions of the album still seem very raw. In promoting *Red*, Swift often seemed less open than she did during interviews for her previous albums, and it is easy to see the strain that the rumors about her personal life and the demands of performance had placed on her.

If *Red* represents the weight of Swift's fame, career, and personal life, *1989* lifts that weight. It was her first true pop album, a complete departure from her country roots, and a major gamble. While her label had expressed doubts about releasing an all-pop record, *1989* was met with huge success, selling 1.287 million copies in the first week, winning the Grammy for Album of the Year, and becoming the bestselling album of 2014 in the United States.

Swift also made the major decision not to release *1989* on Spotify, and she later pulled her entire back catalog from the streaming service. She also wrote a critical open letter to Apple Music after learning that the service wouldn't pay artist royalties for the music streamed during users' three-month free trial. Swift argued that the system was unfair, not just for a huge pop star like her, but for new artists as well. The industry, to some degree, responded—Apple Music agreed to pay its artists during the three-month trial.

Of course, Swift is still a pop star, so even when she speaks up about the music industry or makes major changes in her career, she still carries baggage like silly questions about her dating life and, a few years after *1989*'s release, the controversy that would inspire the next move in her career. After rumored feuding with Kanye West, ex-boyfriend Calvin Harris, and Katy Perry, some saw Swift as a backstabbing diva who uses her fame to ruin other people's careers. Long gone was the innocent, curly-haired teen of the *Taylor Swift* era and the earnest, heartbroken singer on *Red*. But, just like always, Swift was ready—eventually—with a new image that addressed the rumors.

In late 2017, Swift wiped all of her social media accounts, then posted videos of a coiled snake. Soon after, Swift announced her upcoming album *Reputation* and released "Look What You Made Me Do." The lyrics and music video of the single reference her feuds and show her emerging from them harder and meaner than she was before. Swift was taking ownership of her reputation, leaning into it so no one could make fun of her or fight with her anymore. But Swift has never used her music just for making over her own image. Underneath the rougher image of *Reputation* was the emotional heart of the album: songs that show Swift falling in love—likely with long-time beau Joe Alwyn—in the cloud of her reputation.

In the summer of 2019, Swift again teased a new album on social media, this time posting bright, pastel photos before dropping the upbeat pop song "ME!" The album that followed, *Lover*, was a new era and a return to the days of that goofy, girly, emotionally honest teen—and proof that she never really went away. Rather than engage in a global tour, Swift planned to play a few smaller festivals to promote *Lover*, but the onset of the COVID-19 pandemic forced her to cancel all of the shows.

It was during the pandemic that Swift dropped the surprise album *Folklore*, which was doubly surprising because it was yet another departure from her past musical genres, this time turning toward mellow indie folk ballads. These songs were, for the first time, less about her own life and more about fictional characters she imagined. The surprises didn't stop there, though. A few months later she released *Folklore*'s sister album, *Evermore*, a continuation of the indie sounds and fictional story arcs that she said she couldn't stop writing.

The following year, Swift began releasing new recordings of her first six albums, which had been released under her previous label. Big Machine had refused to sell the master recordings back to Swift when her contract ended, and instead sold them to music manager Scooter Braun, whom Swift accused of being a bully. Fans embraced the rereleases, replacing the old ones with the new on their streaming playlists, and critics appeared to support her as well, with Billboard calling her the "Greatest Pop Star of 2021."

In 2022, Swift returned to her pop era with the release of her electropop album *Midnights*, inspired by the anxiety and insecurity of sleepless nights. The album broke numerous records, including the most single-day streams of an album on Spotify, and ten of the songs filled all the top-ten slots on the Billboard Hot 100 in the same week—the first time any album had done so.

After five years of not touring, Swift was overdue for a return to the stage, and it came in the form of her Eras Tour, a five-continent stadium tour that would cover all of her albums and musical eras to date. On the first day of U.S. pre-sales, the Ticketmaster website crashed under the demand of 14 million fans trying to get tickets. Like so many other aspects of Swift's career, the tour would go on to sell out worldwide, break records, and become a cultural phenomenon.

The quotes in this book show Taylor Swift change, fall down, get back up, develop a voice for herself, discover new ideas, and build a legacy, not just as a singer, but as a cultural icon, a voice for artists, and a young woman who has had to grow up quickly but has always kept pace.

Part I

PERSONAL LIFE

Never Grow Up: Early Life and the Road to Nashville

I GREW UP on a Christmas tree farm, and I just remember having all this space to run around and be a crazy kid with tangled hair. And I think that really had a lot to do with me being able to have an imagination and become obsessed with, like, little stories I created in my head. Which then, later in life, led to songwriting.

—rehearsals for the 52nd Annual Grammy Awards,
January 31, 2010

MY MOM THOUGHT it was cool that if you got a business card that said "Taylor" you wouldn't know if it was a guy or a girl. She wanted me to be a business person in a business world.

—*Rolling Stone*, March 5, 2009

WHEN I PICKED up the guitar, I could not stop. I would literally play until my fingers bled—my mom had to tape them up, and you can imagine how popular that made me: "Look at her fingers, so weird."

—*Rolling Stone*, March 5, 2009

I ACTUALLY LEARNED on a twelve-string, purely because some guy told me that I'd never be able to play it, that my fingers were too small. Anytime someone tells me that I can't do something, I want to do it more.

—*Teen Vogue*, **January 26, 2009**

EDITORIAL NOTE: Guitars generally have six or twelve strings. Twelve-string guitars are known for being a bit harder for new players to learn on because they have a wider neck, forcing the player's hand to have to reach farther to press on the strings.

I STARTED WRITING songs because, when I'd have a difficult day at school or I'd be going through a hard time, I'd just tell myself, like, "It's OK, you can write a song about this later." And so I think I trained my brain to be like, "Pain? Write a song about it. Like, intense feeling? Write a song about it."

—*Today* Australia, **November 26, 2012**

WHEN YOU'RE IN school, anything that makes you different makes you weird, and anything [that] makes you weird makes you just off-limits. . . . And I think that you run into that same story line a lot with musicians and people who end up in the music industry or Hollywood or whatever, because they loved something from a very early age that not a lot of other kids loved.

—**Beats 1, December 13, 2015**

I REMEMBER THE girls who would come to talent shows and say to anyone they met, "I'm so-and-so—I'm going to be famous someday." I was never that girl. I would show up with my guitar and say, "This is a song I wrote about a boy in my class." And that's what I still do today.

—*Glamour*, **July 1, 2009**

I THINK THAT the way music can transport you back to a long-forgotten memory is the closest sensation we have to traveling in time. To this day, when I hear "Cowboy Take Me Away" by the Dixie Chicks, I instantly recall the feeling of being twelve years old, sitting in a little wood paneled room in my family home in Pennsylvania.

I'm clutching a guitar and learning to play the chords and sing the words at the same time, rehearsing for a **gig** at a coffee house.

—*Elle* UK, February 28, 2019

GIG (noun): a small, live performance for a musician

EDITORIAL NOTE: The Dixie Chicks are a country music group who, inspired by racial justice protests in 2020, changed their name to The Chicks, dropping the word "Dixie" because it usually refers to the southern states that made up the Confederacy during the American Civil War.

WHEN I WAS ten I saw this TV program about Faith Hill, and it said, you know, "When Faith Hill was nineteen or so she moved to Nashville, and that's how she got into country music." And so I had this **epiphany** when I was ten. I was like, I need to be in Nashville. That's a magical dream world where dreams come true.... That's when I started on my daily begging rant with my parents of, "I need to go to Nashville, please, please, please take me to Nashville. I need to go!"

—*The Paul O'Grady Show*, May 8, 2009

EPIPHANY (noun): realization or discovery

EDITORIAL NOTE: Faith Hill is a country music singer who rose to fame in the early 1990s and found success in both country and pop music, winning three Country Music Association Awards and five Grammy Awards.

IT SOUNDS REALLY crazy to move across the country for your 14-year-old, but I was really **persistent**. And from the time I was about nine years old I was doing theater productions every time I got a chance. I was performing in cafés and writing songs and recording demos. Looking back, I feel a little weird about it because it doesn't seem normal for a kid. But it felt normal to me.

—*Top Billing*, November 7, 2014

PERSISTENT (adj): refusing to give up, set on something

EDITORIAL NOTE: Demos, short for "demonstrations," are early draft versions of songs to give the listener an idea of what the final song might sound like. They're recorded by bands or artists to send to record labels, producers, or anyone else who might help them professionally record or perform the song.

WHEN I WAS 10 years old, I'd lie awake at night and think about the roaring crowd and walking out onstage and that light hitting me for the first time. But I was always very calculated about it. I would think about exactly how I was going to get there, not just how it would feel to be there.

—*Country Weekly*, December 3, 2007

IT TAKES A lot of different stepping stones, and meeting different people who introduce you to this person, and then working really hard. Playing **venues** that aren't even venues. Playing Boy Scout meetings, and garden club meetings, and coffee shops, and anywhere you can, just because you love it.

—*My Date With . . .*, November 13, 2009

VENUES (noun): locations where events (performances, for example) take place

I GOT A job as a songwriter for Sony/ATV Publishing when I was fourteen. . . . I was in eighth grade, and my mom would pick me up from school and drive me downtown, and I would go write songs with these great songwriters in Nashville. And then I'd go home and do my homework.

—*The Ellen DeGeneres Show*, November 11, 2008

I KNEW EVERY writer I wrote with was pretty much going to think, "I'm going to write a song for a 14-year-old today." So I would come into each meeting with 5 to 10 ideas that were solid. I wanted them to look at me as a person they were writing with, not a little kid.

—*New York Times*, November 7, 2008

WHEN I WAS making the rounds first trying to get a record deal, the thing that I heard the most is, "Country music does not have a young **demographic**. The country music demographic is 35-year-old females, and those are the only people that listen to country radio. . . ."

That's what I heard everywhere I went, and I just kept thinking that can't be true. That can't be accurate because I listen to country music and I know there have to be other girls everywhere who listen to country music and want some music that is maybe directed more towards them, toward people our age.

—*CMT Insider*, November 26, 2008

DEMOGRAPHIC (noun): a specific section of the population identified by a common trait

---

ALL THE SONGS I heard on the radio were about marriage and kids and settling down. I just couldn't relate to that. I kept writing songs about the guy who I dated for a couple of weeks and who cheated on me, about all the things I was going through. . . . I felt there was no reason why country music shouldn't relate to someone my age if someone my age was writing it.

—*Telegraph*, **April 26, 2009**

I HAD THIS showcase at The Bluebird Cafe, ironically the place where Faith Hill got discovered. And I played my guitar and sang a bunch of songs that I'd written. There was one guy in the audience named Scott Borchetta. So he came up to me after the show and he said, "I want you on my record label, and I want you to write all your own music," and I was so excited. And I get a call from him later that week and he goes, "Hey, so, good news is I want you on my record label. Bad news is that I don't actually have a record label yet."

—*Taylor Swift: Journey to* **Fearless, October 22, 2010**

EVEN WHEN I go back to high school now, when I go back to functions like a football game or a band concert or something like that, it doesn't matter how many people come up and ask me for my autograph, if I see like one of those popular people, I still feel like my hair is frizzy and people are looking at me.

—*Seventeen*, **January 20, 2009**

ME!:

Becoming

Taylor Swift

I'M KIND OF used to being shot out of a cannon, you know? That's kind of like what my life has become, and it's an **exhilarating** feeling, for sure. And, yeah, you're exhausted, but it's an exhausted feeling with, like, a sense of accomplishment too.

—**Mix 93.3**, October 29, 2012

EXHILARATING (adj.): causing strong feelings of happiness and excitement

---

I NEVER WON anything in school or in sports, and then all of a sudden, I started winning things. People always say, "Live in the moment"—if you really live in the moment at a big awards show and you win, you freak out!

—*Rolling Stone*, October 25, 2012

EDITORIAL NOTE: In 2012, Swift was known for big, excited reactions to winning at awards shows, which were often made into GIFs.

I WAS RAISED by two parents who raised me to never be **presumptuous** about success or winning, and they always would say you have to work for every single thing that you get. And, you know, so every single time I've won an award or something like that, it's been like I win it like it's the last time I'll ever win anything.

—*The Alan Titchmarsh Show*, October 28, 2010

PRESUMPTUOUS (adj): taking things for granted, making assumptions

WORDS ARE EVERYTHING to me. Words can build me up and make me feel so good. And on the flip side, words can absolutely demolish me. I am nowhere close to being bulletproof when it comes to criticism.

—*Entertainment Weekly*, December 3, 2010

MY CONFIDENCE IS easy to shake. I am very well aware of all of my flaws. . . . I have a lot of voices in my head constantly telling me I can't do it. . . . And getting up there on stage thousands of times, you're going to have off nights. And when you have an off night in front of that many people, and it's pointed out in such a public way, yeah, that gets to you. I feel like, as a songwriter, I can't develop thick skin. I cannot put up protective walls, because it's my job to feel things.

—*All Things Considered*, November 2, 2012

I'M **INTIMIDATED** BY the fear of being average.

—Associated Press, November 21, 2006

INTIMIDATED (adj): afraid of or threatened by

I DOUBT MYSELF like four hundred thousand times per ten-minute interval. . . . I have a ridiculously, terrifyingly long list of fears—like, literally everything. Everything. Diseases. Spiders. Like, the support of roofs. Or I get scared of the idea of people, like, getting tired of me in general, which is a broader concept.

—*VH1 Storytellers*, **November 11, 2012**

MY MOM IS the last straw. She is the last-ditch effort for me to feel better because she's really good at being **rational** and realistic. She's going to always bring me back to a place where I'm not so imbalanced.

—*Vanity Fair*, **August 11, 2015**

RATIONAL (adj): reasonable or logical

I'M REALLY NOT interested in, like, an **entourage** of people who tell me what I want to hear all the time. That doesn't thrill me or excite me at all. I have friends who are all passionate about what they do. They all have their own lives, their own jobs, their own things that they're obsessed with like I'm obsessed with music.

—BBC Radio 1, October 9, 2014

ENTOURAGE (noun): group of people who surround someone and assist them with their needs

---

I HONESTLY THINK my lack of female friendships in high school and middle school is why my female friendships are so important now. Because I always wanted them. It was just hard for me to have friends.

—*GQ*, October 15, 2015

WE EVEN HAVE girls in our group who have dated the same people. It's almost like the sisterhood has such a higher place on the list of priorities for us.... When you've got this group of girls who need each other as much as we need each other, in this climate, when it's so hard for women to be understood and portrayed the right way in the media ... now more than ever we need to be good and kind to each other and not judge each other—and just because you have the same taste in men, we don't hold that against each other.

—*Vanity Fair*, August 11, 2015

I'VE ALWAYS FELT, you know, 40, in my career sensibilities and things like that. I've had to grow up fast. But then I think on the opposite end that's kind of stunted my maturity as far as, like, my interests and my hobbies. My ideal Fourth of July celebration was creating a giant slip and slide on my lawn.

—behind the scenes of *Lucky* cover shoot,
December 2014

A LL I THINK about are metaphors and cats.

—Yahoo! live stream, August 18, 2014

M Y CATS ARE named after my favorite female lead TV show characters. My first cat is named Meredith after Meredith Grey. My second cat is named Olivia after Detective Olivia Benson. Let's set the record straight: I'm not getting a third cat because, you know, two cats is a party, three cats is a cat lady. But if I *were* to—you know, you *have* to get another cat, you *have* to name it something—I might name it Monica Geller.

—behind the scenes of *Lucky* cover shoot,
December 2014

EDITORIAL NOTE: Meredith Grey is the lead character in the medical drama *Grey's Anatomy*. Olivia Benson is the name of the lead detective in *Law & Order: Special Victims Unit*, and Monica Geller is one of the six main characters in the sitcom *Friends*. In 2019, Swift did get a third cat, naming him Benjamin Button.

I'M VERY ORGANIZED in weird ways, and I kind of like to be able to look at old pictures and see what my hair looks like and what I'm wearing and be like, "Oh, that was the second album!"

—**Yahoo! live stream, August 18, 2014**

I'LL HAVE THESE style epiphanies. When I was fifteen, I realized that I loved the idea of a dress—like a sundress—and cowboy boots. And that's all I wore for, like, two years. And then I just started loving the bohemian, like, fairy-type look . . . so I dressed like a fairy would dress for like two years. And now I see pictures from the '50s and '60s where women had, like, red lips and a pearl earring and, like, those very classic looks. And I kind of dress now a little more **vintage**-y. So it's always got a direction to it.

—**Keds partnership video, May 15, 2013**

> **VINTAGE** (adj): aged or antique

I'M NEVER GONNA have the moment where I'm like, "I'm a woman now, guys. I'm only gonna write dark songs and I'm gonna dance in my bra all the time." Like, I just—that's not really me. I hope things will gradually evolve into growing up kind of as people naturally grow up.

—*Today*, February 14, 2012

WE'RE TAUGHT TO find examples for the way we want our lives to wind up. But I can't find anyone, really, who's had the same career **trajectory** as mine. So when I'm in an optimistic place I hope that my life won't match anyone else's life trajectory, either, going forward.

—*Time*, November 13, 2014

TRAJECTORY (noun): path

I GET SO ahead of myself. I'm like, "What am I going to be doing at 30?" But there's no way to know that! So it's this endless mind-boggling equation that you'll never figure out. I overanalyze myself into being a big bag of worries.

—*Vogue*, January 16, 2012

WE'RE PEOPLE-PLEASERS, THAT'S why we became entertainers, so if people don't want you to be on stage anymore in sparkly dresses singing songs to teenagers when I'm 40, then I'm just not going to do it. It's just a goal of mine to not try and be something I'm not.

—*Vogue* Australia, November 14, 2015

My LIFE WOULD kind of go, like, you record an album, you put out the album, you go on tour.... And it kind of went like that over and over again until I finished with the *1989* World Tour. And I just felt like I needed to kind of stop for a second and think about who I would be as a person if I broke that kind of cycle of constantly making something and putting it out—like, if I stopped to reflect. What kind of life would I have if there wasn't a spotlight on that life? And I was a little afraid to do that because I was like, "Oh my God. What if they don't wanna hang out with me anymore? They'll forget about me, they're gonna move on, go see someone else who wears sparkly dresses, I don't know." And I was so honored and pleasantly surprised that you guys were so supportive of me taking a break. You're so **empathetic**. You guys were like, "Go, be happy! We just want you to be happy!"

—*Reputation* **Stadium Tour, Foxborough, Massachusetts, July 26, 2018**

EMPATHETIC (adj): able to understand and be sensitive to the feelings or thoughts of another person

EVERY PART OF you that you've ever been, every phase you've ever gone through, was you working it out in that moment with the information you had available to you at the time. There's a lot that I look back at like, "Wow, a couple years ago I might have cringed at this." You should celebrate who you are now, where you're going, and where you've been.

—*Time*, December 6, 2023

Love Story:

Romance,

Heartbreak,

and

Reputation

I'M FASCINATED BY love rather than the principle of "Oh, does this guy like me?" I love love. I love studying it and watching it. I love thinking about how we treat each other, and the crazy way that one person can feel one thing and another can feel totally different.

—*Rolling Stone*, March 5, 2009

WHEN PEOPLE NEED music the most is when they're either falling in love or falling out of it.

—backstage at the 2012 Canadian Country Music Association Awards, September 9, 2012

I WROTE ["Teardrops on My Guitar"] about a guy that I had a crush on, and he didn't know. Inevitably, he knows now. And, you know, I have this habit of writing songs about guys and naming them. I can't seem to stop doing that.

—*The Paul O'Grady Show*, May 8, 2009

I JUST FIGURE if guys don't want me to write bad songs about them they shouldn't do bad things.

—*Dateline*, **May 31, 2009**

I THINK I fall into the category of the hopeless romantics, and I think that you do too, because you're here. The tricky thing about us, the tricky thing about the hopeless romantics, is that when we fall in love with someone, when we say hello, and it's magical, we never imagine that that hello could someday turn into a goodbye. And when we have our first kiss with someone and it's magical, we never, ever imagine that someday that could turn into a last kiss.

—**Speak Now** *World Tour Live*, **November 21, 2011**

I HAVE A lot of rules placed on my life, and I just choose not to apply rules to love.

—*The Jonathan Ross Show*, October 6, 2012

I THINK I am smart unless I am really, really in love, and then I am ridiculously stupid.

—*Vogue*, January 16, 2012

MY EXPERIENCES IN love have taught me difficult lessons, especially my experiences with crazy love. The red relationships. The ones that went from zero to a hundred miles per hour and then hit a wall and exploded. And it was awful. And ridiculous. And desperate. And thrilling. And when the dust settled, it was something I'd never take back.

—*Red* liner notes, October 22, 2012

I'D NEVER BEEN in a relationship when I wrote my first couple of albums, so these were all projections of what I thought they might be like. They were based on movies and books and songs and literature that tell us that a relationship is the most magical thing that can ever happen to you. And then once I fell in love, or thought I was in love, and then experienced disappointment or it just not working out a few times, I realized there's this idea of happily ever after which in real life doesn't happen. There's no riding off into the sunset, because the camera always keeps rolling in real life.

—*Elle*, May 7, 2015

OVER THE YEARS, I think, as you get more experience under your belt, as you become disappointed a few times, you start to kind of think of things in more realistic terms. It's not, you meet someone and that's it, you know. If they like you and you like them, well, it's gonna be forever, of course. I don't really look at love like that anymore. I think the way I see love is a little more **fatalistic**, which means to me that when I meet someone and we have a connection, the first thought I really have is, "When this is over, I hope you think well of me."

—**"Wildest Dreams" commentary, *1989* (Big Machine Radio Release Special), December 13, 2018**

FATALISTIC (adj): believing future events are fixed and humans can't change them

---

IF YOU FELT something, it was worth it and it happened for a reason. And for me, when I play songs that are happy songs but I don't really know that person anymore, I still feel happy. Like, it's celebrating that it existed at one point, you know?

—VH1 Storytellers, **November 11, 2012**

A LETDOWN IS worth a few songs. A heartbreak is worth a few albums.

—Elle, **March 4, 2010**

WHEN YOU'RE TRULY heartbroken you're never like, "Yes! I can **parlay** this into something!" You're like, "I wanna stay in bed for five years and just eat ice cream." But I don't know, I don't think that I've ever, like, celebrated a breakup like, "Now I've got new material!" But it just kind of ends up happening that way.

—*Elvis Duran and the Morning Show*, July 22, 2011

> **PARLAY** (verb): to turn one thing into something else more
> desirable

YOU CAN HAVE the most pointless relationship, and, if you write a great song about it, it was worthwhile.

—**Digital Rodeo video, April 15, 2009**

I HEARD FROM the guy that most of *Red* is about. He was like, "I just listened to the album, and that was a really bittersweet experience for me. It was like going through a photo album." That was nice. Nicer than, like, the ranting, crazy e-mails I got from this one dude. It's a lot more mature way of looking at a love that was wonderful until it was terrible, and both people got hurt from it—but one of those people happened to be a songwriter.

—*New York*, November 25, 2013

MY GIRLFRIENDS AND I are plagued by the idea, looking back, that [some boys] changed us. You look back and you think: I only wore black in that relationship. Or I started speaking differently. Or I started trying to act like a hipster. Or I cut off my friends and family because he wanted me to do that. It's an unfortunate problem.

—*Guardian*, October 18, 2012

["We Are Never Ever Getting Back Together"]
kind of makes a breakup sound like a party. You
know, there are so many different ways a breakup
could sound, but one of the ways is like, "Yes!
Celebration! We're done!"

—*Extra*, October 23, 2012

MY PREVIOUS ALBUMS [before *1989*] have always
been sort of like, "I was right, you were wrong.
You did this; it made me feel like this." Kind of
a sense of righteous, like, right and wrong in a
relationship. And what happens when you grow
up is you realize that the rules in a relationship
are very, very blurred, and that it gets very
complicated very quickly, and there's not always
a case of who was right and who was wrong.

—*On Air with Ryan Seacrest*, October 31, 2014

IN THE LAST couple of years the story has been that I'm, like, a serial dater, and I, like, have all these boyfriends and we're traveling around the world and everything's great, until I get overemotional and crazy and obsessive and then they leave. And I'm devastated, and then I write songs to get emotional revenge because I'm psychotic. And, you know, that character, if you think about it, if that's actually how I was, is such a complex, interesting character to write from the perspective of.... If you make the joke first and you make the joke better, then it's kind of like it's not as funny when other people call you a name.

—on "Blank Space," *The Morning Show*, December 29, 2014

EDITORIAL NOTE: The media often focused more on Swift's dating habits than her music, and the song "Blank Space" represents Swift's attempt to take back the narrative and make a joke about the type of person they made her out to be.

THEY ALWAYS GO to the same **fabricated** ending that every other tabloid has used in my story, which is, "She got too clingy," or "Taylor has too many emotions, she scared him away." Which has honestly never been the reason for any of my break-ups. You know what has been the reason? The media. You take something very fragile, like trying to get to know someone, and it feels like walking out into the middle of a gladiator arena with someone you've just met.

—*Glamour* UK, April 24, 2015

FABRICATED (adj): made-up or invented

I REALLY DIDN'T like the whole serial-dater thing. I thought it was a really sexist angle on my life. And so I just stopped dating people, because it meant a lot to me to set the record straight— that I do not need some guy around in order to get inspiration, in order to make a great record, in order to live my life, in order to feel okay about myself.

—*Esquire*, October 20, 2014

I'll say, "Things are great" but what's interesting is the first thing people say to you is, "Don't worry, you'll find someone."

—the *Sun*, October 27, 2014

If someone doesn't seem to want to get to know me as a person but instead seems to have kind of bought into the whole idea of me and he approves of my Wikipedia page? And falls in love based on zero hours spent with me? That's maybe something to be aware of. That will fade fast. You can't be in love with a Google search.

—*Vogue*, January 16, 2012

WHEN I'M GETTING to know someone, I look for someone who has passions that I respect, like his career. Someone who loves what he does is really attractive. In high school, I used to think it was "like sooooo cool" if a guy had an awesome car. Now none of that matters. These days I look for character and honesty and trust.

—*Glamour*, October 5, 2010

I DON'T THINK love is ever gonna be perfect. And I think that when you actually are in a long relationship and you have to sustain it and work at it, I think that's a very real thing. And it's not all pretty and sparkly and fairy tale–esque and, you know, it doesn't really have the stamp of, like, Prince Charming. But I think that he would listen to you at the end of a hard day and I think that he'd be there for you and feel like a teammate.

—*Elvis Duran and the Morning Show*, July 22, 2011

REAL LOVE DOESN'T mess with your head. Real love just is. Real love just endures. Real love maintains. Real love takes it page by page.

—*Vogue*, **April 14, 2016**

Part II

EMPIRE BUILDER

Blank Space:

Inside the

Music

SONGWRITING HAS ALWAYS been the number one thing. . . . If I didn't write, I wouldn't sing.

—*CBS This Morning*, October 29, 2014

MUSIC IS THE only thing that's ever fit me like that little black dress you wear every single time you go out. Other things fit me for certain seasons, but music is the only thing that I would wear all year round.

—*Esquire*, October 20, 2014

I DIDN'T WANT to just be another girl singer. I wanted there to be something that set me apart. And I knew that had to be my writing.

—*Entertainment Weekly*, July 25, 2007

I'VE ALWAYS KNOWN that [writing] was the main pillar holding up my career. I've always known it was the main pillar of kind of my sanity as well.

—Time 100 Gala, April 23, 2019

WHEN I WAS twelve years old and I started writing songs, I hadn't been in relationships! I would just think about the movies I had watched and the most memorable scenes and when they're standing in the rain and this girl had no idea that this guy had feelings for her this entire time and she thought that he liked that other girl, but really he liked her. And there's a moment that happens in movies that I try to capture in songs. It's **cinematic**; it's emotional.

—*VH1 Storytellers*, November 11, 2012

CINEMATIC (adj): like a movie

IT'S NOT ... heartbreak that inspires my songs. It's not love that inspires my songs. It's individual people that come into my life. I've had relationships with people that were really substantial and meant a lot to me, but I couldn't write a song about that person for some reason. Then again, you'll meet someone that comes into your life for two weeks and you write an entire record about them.

—All Things Considered, **November 2, 2012**

I LOVE WRITING songs because I love preserving memories, like putting a picture frame around a feeling you once had.

—Elle **UK, February 28, 2019**

I'VE ALWAYS LOOKED at writing as sort of a protective armor, which is weird because . . . writing about your life [is] usually likened to **vulnerability**. But I think that when you write about your life, it gives you the ability to process your life. I use it as a way of justifying things that happened to me, whether they're good or bad. You know, I like to honor the good times and really process the bad times when I write.

—Time 100 Gala, April 23, 2019

VULNERABILITY (noun): a quality of emotional openness that often reveals a person's fears or weaknesses

MY ADVICE TO first-time songwriters would be, know the person you're writing the song about. First know that. And then write a letter to them, like what you would say if you could. Because, you know, that's why I listen to music, is because it says how I feel better than I could, and it says what I wish I'd said when that moment was there.

—live chat with fans, July 20, 2010

I USED TO think that if you leave out details that people could relate more. But I don't think that's the case, because I think that it's really the more you let people in, the more they feel let in, and the more they feel like we all share something.

—*Extra*, February 15, 2012

I THINK THESE days, people are reaching out for connection and comfort in the music they listen to. We like being confided in and hearing someone say, "this is what I went through" as proof to us that we can get through our own struggles.

We actually do NOT want our pop music to be generic. I think a lot of music lovers want some biographical glimpse into the world of our narrator, a hole in the emotional walls people put up around themselves to survive.

—*Elle* UK, February 28, 2019

SINCE I WAS twelve, I would get an idea, and that idea is either a fragment of melody and lyric mixed in, [or] maybe it's a hook. Maybe it's the first line of a song. Maybe it's a background vocal part or something, but it's like the first piece of a puzzle. And my job in writing the song and completing it is filling in all the rest of the pieces and figuring out where they go.

—*All Things Considered*, November 2, 2012

EDITORIAL NOTE: A "hook" in a song is often the title of the song, or another lyric that is repeated throughout the song, usually as part of the chorus. This snippet, both the lyrics and the melody, makes the song memorable, recognizable, and unique.

CREATIVITY IS GETTING inspiration and having that lightning bolt idea moment, and then having the hard **work ethic** to sit down at the desk and write it down.

—*Vogue*, "73 Questions with Taylor Swift," April 19, 2016

WORK ETHIC (noun): set of beliefs around hard work and determination

---

THERE ARE MYSTICAL, magical moments, **inexplicable** moments when an idea that is fully formed just pops into your head. And that's the purest part of my job. It can get complicated on every other level, but the songwriting is still the same uncomplicated process it was when I was 12 years old writing songs in my room.

—*Harper's Bazaar*, July 10, 2018

INEXPLICABLE (adj): impossible to explain

WHEN I GET an idea, it happens really fast, and I need to record it really fast into whatever I have, either a cell phone or write it on something. And so I was walking through an airport and I got an idea and I needed to write it on something, and I knew there were paper towels in the bathroom. So, [I] ran into the bathroom, started writing it down, ran back out to the terminal, and finished the song, only to realize it was the men's bathroom that I had run into.

—*The Jay Leno Show*, December 4, 2009

THE MOMENT IN the day when I get the most
ideas is when I'm about to go to sleep because,
from the time I wake up till that moment, I'm
thinking about things nonstop. I'm thinking
about what I need to get done that day, I'm
thinking about, you know, what decisions I need
to make that are gonna affect everything. So
before I go to bed, that's the one time when I'm
just thinking about ideas, and stuff usually hits
me then.

—**Digital Rodeo video, April 15, 2009**

IF I'M PUTTING together an album and half of my
brain is like, "This is so great!" there's another
half of my brain that's poking holes in every part
of it going, "What are people who hate you gonna
say about this song? Are they gonna like it? You
need to write a song so good even people who
hate you get it stuck in their head."

—**behind the scenes of *Vogue* Australia cover shoot,
October 18, 2015**

I THINK IF I had to put a color to *Speak Now*, it would be purple. I think that there's just something kind of . . . honest and true about that record that kind of, to me, seems purple. And *Fearless*, to me, is golden because it was, you know, the first time that anyone really recognized my music outside of America, and to me that was like a golden rush of something new. My first album, I think, would be blue.

—**Universal Music Korea video, October 23, 2012**

EDITORIAL NOTE: Much of Swift's fanbase now considers her first album to be green-coded rather than blue, likely due to her using light blue in the promotional materials for her *1989* album and dark blue for the *Midnights* album. Official merchandise and apparel for the Eras Tour also codes her debut era as green.

I HAD A lot of people who would say, "Oh, she's an 18-year-old girl. There's no way that she actually carried her weight in those writing sessions." And that was a really harsh criticism I felt because, you know, there was no way I could prove them wrong other than to write my entire next record solo. So I went in and I made an album called *Speak Now*. There is not one single cowriter on the entire thing.

—*Taylor Swift—Road to* **Reputation, September 28, 2018**

THIS ONE REALLY means a lot to me because this is for a song called "Mean" that I wrote. And there's really no feeling quite like writing a song about someone who's really mean to you and someone who completely hates you and makes your life miserable and then winning a Grammy for it.

—**54th Annual Grammy Awards, February 12, 2012**

EDITORIAL NOTE: At the 2010 Grammy Awards, Swift performed on stage with singer-songwriter Stevie Nicks, and she was widely criticized for singing off-key, which Swift reported was due to stage fright. One critic's harsh words inspired her to write the song "Mean."

I'M USED TO being called too something. From my first album, I've been called either, you know, "This is too pop," "This is too rock." I had a song called "Mean" that people said was too bluegrass, too country, which I thought was funny. And I kind of had this **revelation** that I don't mind it if people are calling my music too something. It's people saying that all my songs are starting to sound the same—that's the big fear.

—VH1 Storytellers, **November 11, 2012**

REVELATION (noun): realization

RED STARTED OUT, I was making country music. And I was getting the ideas exactly the same way I always did, and they were coming to me in the same ways. And then, a few months in, they started coming to me as pop melodies, and I could not fight it, and I just embraced it.

—Taylor Swift—Road to **Reputation, September 28, 2018**

I LOVE THE color red for the title because, if you correlate red with, you know, different emotions, you come up with the most intense ones. On this side you've got, like, passion and falling in love, and that intrigue and adventure and daring. And then on the other side you've got, like, anger and jealousy and frustration and betrayal.

—*MTV News* UK, October 6, 2012

I LIKE TO balance out the amount of happy songs, breakup songs, sentimental songs, I-miss-you songs, angry songs. I don't want to try and harp on the same emotion too much because I feel like if you make the "angry" album, that's going to lose people.

—*Elle*, June 15, 2009

THERE ARE ELEMENTS of darkness in our everyday life. There are elements of kind of these darker emotions, and we have to just figure out how to get through them or shine a light on them or look at them a different way, just in order to survive and be happy and be content. But in my songwriting, a lot of the time I'll have kind of a darker message with a lighter, happier beat or melody and just **juxtapose** them because I like the way that that feels.

—*Big Morning Buzz Live*, October 27, 2014

JUXTAPOSE (verb): place two things in contrast with one another

THE WILD, UNPREDICTABLE fun in making music today is that anything goes. Pop sounds like hip hop; country sounds like rock; rock sounds like soul; and folk sounds like country—and to me, that's incredible progress. I want to make music that reflects all of my influences, and I think that in the coming decades the idea of genres will become less of a career-defining path and more of an organizational tool.

—*Wall Street Journal*, July 7, 2014

WE DON'T MAKE music so we can, like, win a lot of awards, but you have to take your cues from somewhere if you're gonna continue to evolve. You have a few options when you don't win an award. You can decide, like, "Oh, they're wrong. They all voted wrong." Second, you can be like, "I'm gonna go up on the stage and take the mic from whoever did win it." Or, third, you can say, "Maybe they're right. Maybe I did not make the record of my career. Maybe I need to fix the problem, which was that I have not been making sonically cohesive albums. I need to really think about whether I'm listening to the record label and what that's doing to the art I'm making."

—**Grammy listening sessions, October 9, 2015**

> **EDITORIAL NOTE:** "Sonically cohesive" means that all the songs on the album fit together because they have a similar style. The album *Red* was criticized for not being sonically cohesive because it was intended as a country album but often crossed over into more pop-like melodies.

I THINK THAT if you're chasing a trend, by the time you put that music out, the trend is going to be over and there's going to be sort of a new wave of what's working. And I think I'd much rather kind of be part of a new wave and create something new rather than try to chase what everyone else is doing at the time.

—KISS FM UK, October 9, 2014

THERE'S A MISTAKE that I see artists make when they're on their fourth or fifth record, and they think **innovation** is more important than solid songwriting. The most terrible letdown as a listener for me is when I'm listening to a song and I see what they were trying to do. Like, where there's a dance break that doesn't make any sense, there's a rap that shouldn't be there, there's like a beat change that's, like, the coolest, hippest thing this six months—but it has nothing to do with the feeling, it has nothing to do with the emotion, it has nothing to do with the lyric.

—*New York*, November 25, 2013

INNOVATION (noun): the creation or invention of something new

I REALLY LIKE to explore the edges of what I'm allowed to do. And I don't like to think that there are ceilings for what we're allowed to do musically. I think that if you don't play using different instruments, if you don't paint using different colors, you're making the choice to stay the same.

—*VH1 Storytellers*, **November 11, 2012**

IT FEELS AMAZING to have so much control over my career and so much creative control over what the record looks like, how it sounds, what songs end up making the album. I'm very lucky, you know, to get to have all those choices up to me.

—**Mix 93.3, October 26, 2012**

I LIKE TO take two years to make an album, so the first year is a lot of experimentation. And it's just sort of like, I'll try out all kinds of different things, and write this kind of song and that kind of song. And after a while you start to naturally **gravitate** towards one thing. And that's what happened with [*1989*], and the thing I naturally gravitated towards was sort of like late 80s–infused synth-pop.

—BBC Radio 1, October 9, 2014

GRAVITATE (verb): to be drawn to a person, place, or idea

EDITORIAL NOTE: Synth-pop is a type of music that was popular in the 1980s. It relies on synthesizers, or electronic musical instruments that often look like electronic keyboards, to create different sounds and textures.

WHEN I KNEW the album had hit its stride, I went to Scott Borchetta and said, "I have to be honest with you: I did not make a country album. I did not make any **semblance** of a country album." And of course he went into a state of semi-panic and went through all the stages of grief—the pleading, the denial. "Can you give me three country songs? Can we put a fiddle on 'Shake It Off'?" And all my answers were a very firm "no," because it felt **disingenuous** to try to exploit two genres when your album falls in only one.

—*Billboard*, December 5, 2014

SEMBLANCE (noun): appearance or resemblance

DISINGENUOUS (adj): dishonest or not sincere

WHAT MY FANS in general were afraid of was
that I would start making pop music and I would
stop writing smart lyrics, or I would stop writing
emotional lyrics. And when they heard the new
music they realized that that wasn't the case at all.

—"Barbara Walters Presents: The 10 Most Fascinating
People of 2014," December 15, 2014

SOMEBODY ONCE TOLD me that you truly see
who a person is when you tell them something
they don't want to hear. . . . To the country music
community, when I told you that I had made a
pop album and that I wanted to go explore other
genres, you showed me who you are with the
grace that you accepted that with.

—50th Annual Academy of Country Music Awards,
April 19, 2015

I THINK WHAT I loved about country music, and what I will always love about it, is that it is such a storytelling genre. You start a story, you tell the second part of the story, and then you finish the story at the end of the song, and you feel like you've been on a lyrical journey. And that is a part of my songwriting that's never gonna leave.

—*Tout le monde en parle*, September 28, 2014

WHEN YOU'RE MAKING pop, you can make a hook out of different elements that I wasn't able to do previously, and that has been thrilling for me as a songwriter. You can shout, speak, whisper—if it's clever enough, it can be a hook.

—*Billboard*, October 24, 2014

THERE'S A SONG called "Love Story" that I wrote when I was seventeen. I'm going to be playing that as long as I'm playing concerts. And I can go back and I can connect to that song—because of the stories I've heard from fans saying, "We walked down the aisle to that song," or how special I feel it was when that was our first No. 1 worldwide hit. But "Tim McGraw," that song I don't really connect to as much. I connect to it in the form of **nostalgia**, but that was a song about a first love. I'm in a very different place in my life right now, and I think you can only hope to grow so much, emotionally, that you can't necessarily connect to wide-eyed fifteen-year-old ideas of love anymore.

—All Things Considered, October 31, 2014

NOSTALGIA (noun): feeling of longingly looking back on a memory

I LIKE TO look at albums as being sort of statements. Visually, sonically, emotionally, I like them all to have their own fingerprint. This time [on *1989*] I'm kind of just doing whatever I feel like. I felt like making a pop album, so I did. I felt like being very honest and unapologetic about it, so I did. I felt like moving to New York—I had no reason to, it wasn't for love or business—so I did. I felt like cutting my hair short, so I did that, too. All these things are in keeping with living my life on my own terms.

—*Billboard*, October 24, 2014

[REPUTATION] WAS DIFFERENT because I kind of built it out from the concept of a reputation. So there are a lot of kind of like, "I'm angry at my reputation" moments. There are [moments] like, "I don't care about my reputation. I'm fine, OK! I don't care!" And then there are these moments where it's very like, "Oh my God, what if my reputation actually makes the person that I like not want to get to know me?"

—Taylor Swift NOW secret show, June 28, 2018

"ME!" IS A song about embracing your individuality and really celebrating it and owning it. And, you know, I think that with a pop song we have the ability to get a melody stuck in people's heads, and I just want it to be one that makes them feel better about themselves, not worse.

—NFL Draft 2019, April 25, 2019

IN ISOLATION MY imagination has run wild and this album [*Folklore*] is the result, a collection of songs and stories that flowed like a stream of consciousness. Picking up a pen was my way of escaping into fantasy, history, and memory. I've told these stories to the best of my ability with all the love, wonder, and whimsy they deserve.

—Instagram post, July 23, 2020

EDITORIAL NOTE: Stream of consciousness is a style of writing that tries to mimic the way the human brain often jumps from one unrelated, incomplete thought to the next, rather than in a straight, logical line.

MY WORLD FELT opened up creatively. There was a point that I got to as a writer who only wrote very **diaristic** songs that I felt it was unsustainable for my future moving forward. So what I felt after we put out *Folklore* was like "Oh wow, people are into this too, this thing that feels really good for my life and feels really good for my creativity . . . it feels good for them too?"

—**Apple Music, December 15, 2020**

DIARISTIC (adj): in the style of a diary, personal

To PUT IT plainly, we just couldn't stop writing songs. To try and put it more poetically, it feels like we were standing on the edge of the folklorian woods and had a choice: to turn and go back or to travel further into the forest of this music. . . . In the past I've always treated albums as one-off eras and moved onto planning the next one as soon as an album was released. There was something different with folklore. In making it, I felt less like I was departing and more like I was returning. I loved the escapism I found in these imaginary/not imaginary tales. I loved the ways you welcomed the dreamscapes and tragedies and epic tales of love lost and found. So I just kept writing them.

—**Instagram post, December 10, 2020**

[*MIDNIGHTS*] IS A pretty dark album, but I'd say I had more fun making it than any album I've ever made. Because I don't think that art and suffering have to be holding hands all the time. I think you can write songs about pain or grief or suffering or loss. . . . But I think with time and with the more albums I put out, making albums and making things and writing things feels like a way to sort of suck the poison out of a snakebite.

—*The Tonight Show Starring Jimmy Fallon,*
October 24, 2022

Long Live:

Taylor's

Greatest

Romance—

with Her

Fans

WHEN I WAS younger and I would write songs in my bedroom, the first thing I would feel was fear, because I was afraid that no one would ever hear it. I can't thank the fans enough, because I don't have to feel that way anymore.

—**CMT Artists of the Year 2010, December 3, 2010**

YOU CAN HAVE, like, a bad day right up until the point where you go onstage, but the second you hear the screams of like twenty thousand people, you're like, "This day isn't that bad. It's gonna be OK."

—**94.9 The Bull, June 20, 2011**

THAT'S THE DIFFERENCE between a singer and a performer. A singer sings for themselves and a performer performs for everyone else.

—***The Voice*, November 3, 2014**

I REALLY JUST thought that I was writing about my life, but what I really didn't understand was that the second I put it out, it was gonna be playing in other girls' bedrooms and playing in the cars of people I had never met before. And when that happens . . . I think you start to realize that as human beings, all we really want is a connection with someone else. And I think that music is that ultimate connection. You know, what if you've got no connection with anybody else? You can always turn to music and you can know that somebody else has gone through it and that you're not alone.

—"Invisible" commentary, *Taylor Swift* (Big Machine Radio Release Special), December 13, 2018

PEOPLE ALWAYS TALK to you about marriages and relationships, and they say relationships take work, and you have to keep surprising each other.... I think the most **profound** relationship I've ever had has been with my fans. That relationship takes work, and you have to continue to think of new ways to delight and surprise them. You can't just assume that because they liked one of your albums, they're going to like the new one, so you can make it exactly the same as you made the last one. You can't just assume that because they were **gracious** enough to make you a part of their life last year, that they're gonna want to do the same thing this year. I think that core relationship needs to be nurtured.

—Yahoo!, November 6, 2014

PROFOUND (adj): deep or insightful

GRACIOUS (adj): kind and generous

WHEN I MEET my fans, it's not like meeting a
stranger. It's sort of like saying hello to someone
that I already know is on the same page with me.

—"CMA Music Festival: Country's Night to Rock" press
conference, August 9, 2011

THERE'S MORE OF a friendship element to
it than anything else. Maybe it's a big-sister
relationship. Or it's a *Hey, we're the same age*—
and we were both 16 when my first album came
out, and we've both grown up together.

—*New York*, November 25, 2013

YOU MIGHT THINK a meet-and-greet with 150 people sounds sad, because maybe you think I'm forced to do it. But you would be surprised. A meaningful conversation doesn't mean that conversation has to last an hour. A meet-and-greet might sound weird to someone who's never done one, but after ten years, you learn to appreciate happiness when it happens, and that happiness is rare and fleeting, and that you're not entitled to it.

—*GQ*, October 15, 2015

EDITORIAL NOTE: Many performers will hold meet-and-greets after a performance, inviting a select group of fans to come backstage to shake hands, chat for a minute or two, or take a photo together. Fans sometimes win a meet-and-greet pass in a contest or purchase it as part of a ticket package.

WE LIKE TO reward people who are in the back rows, or people who didn't think they had a chance to say hi to me at the show, people who brought signs and dressed up and make puffy-paint T-shirts and go crazy. It's almost like a spirit award. We round them up and we bring them backstage for a party after the show.

—*Daily Beast*, October 22, 2012

WHAT I'M BATTLING in this day and age is that every person in the audience probably knows what costumes I'm gonna wear, and they could know the set list if they really wanted to. So I decided to start inviting special guests out. Getting people to say yes to come up onstage was a lot easier than I thought. I'd never want to pressure anybody. I'd never go, "Come on, come on!" But people start to realize before they even got there that if they were to walk out onstage, the crowd's gonna freak out, and they're gonna scream, and it's gonna be an amazing moment for everyone involved.

—*The* 1989 *World Tour Live*, December 20, 2015

I DID THIS thing called the 1989 Secret Sessions a few months ago, way before the album came out. I had spent months picking fans on Instagram, Tumblr, Twitter—people who had been so supportive and had tried and tried to meet me. . . . And in every single one of my houses in the U.S. and my hotel room in London, I would invite eighty-nine people over to my living room, play them the entire album, tell them the stories behind it. And I'd say, you know, you can share your experience, but please keep the secrets about this album a secret.

—*All Things Considered*, October 31, 2014

EDITORIAL NOTE: After Swift held the Secret Sessions for *1989*, she continued the tradition, repeating the experience for select fans before the release of both *Reputation* and *Lover*. The pandemic kept her from being able to do so for *Folklore* and *Evermore*.

WHEN I PICK people to send packages to, I go on their social-media sites for the last six months and figure out what they like or what they are going through. Do they like photography? I'll get them a 1980s Polaroid camera. Do they like **vintage** stuff? I'll go to an antiques place and get them 1920s earrings. . . . When you actually get to know them on a person-by-person basis, you realise what you're doing is special and sacred and it matters.

—*Telegraph*, May 23, 2015

MY FANS MAKE fun of me—it's really cool. They have all these Gifs of me making an idiot of myself or tripping and falling on stage. They bring humour back into it for me. I get too serious sometimes . . . and they bring me back to like, "OK, I'm not really doing anything that difficult. I just need to calm down."

—*Telegraph*, May 23, 2015

EVERYTHING I DID was for [my fans], and I didn't need to try and get every headline or try to get the cover of this or the cover of that. Like, I just needed to think of ways to reach out to them in ways I hadn't even thought of before. So the relationship between me and my fans really actually strengthened throughout the course of *Reputation,* and that was what made it something that I think I'll look back on and find to be one of the most beautiful times of my life, was when I realized that, like, it's me and it's them, and that's what makes this fun for me.

—Beats 1, May 1, 2019

[FANS] HAD TO work really hard to get the tickets. I wanted to play a show that was longer than they ever thought it would be, because that makes me feel good leaving the stadium. . . . I know I'm going on that stage whether I'm sick, injured, heartbroken, uncomfortable, or stressed. That's part of my identity as a human being now. If someone buys a ticket to my show, I'm going to play it unless we have some sort of **force majeure**.

—on the Eras Tour, *Time*, December 6, 2023

FORCE MAJEURE (noun): a big, unavoidable, unforeseeable event

EDITORIAL NOTE: The Eras Tour set list runs over three hours and fifteen minutes long and includes forty-four songs (some of which are shortened versions). By comparison, on the *Reputation* tour, Swift performed about twenty-four tracks over the course of roughly two hours.

Everything Has Changed:

The Shifting Music Industry

I'M VERY WELL aware that the music industry is changing and it will continue to change. And I am open to that change. I am open to progress. I am not open to the financial model that is currently in place. I really believe that we in the music industry can work together to find a way to bond technology with integrity.

—2014 *Billboard* Women in Music Awards,
December 12, 2014

EDITORIAL NOTE: The financial model Swift refers to here is the modern streaming trend, where albums are streamed by listeners rather than purchased, and artists are paid a very small amount per stream, usually less than a cent.

MUSIC IS ART, and art is important and rare. Important, rare things are valuable. Valuable things should be paid for. It's my opinion that music should not be free, and my prediction is that individual artists and their labels will someday decide what an album's price point is. I hope they don't underestimate themselves or undervalue their art.

—*Wall Street Journal*, July 7, 2014

FOR ANYONE WHO wants to create music, for any little kid who's taking piano lessons right now, I want them to have an industry to go into.

—Beats 1, December 13, 2015

EVERYTHING NEW, LIKE Spotify, all feels to me a bit like a grand experiment. And I'm not willing to contribute my life's work to an experiment that I don't feel fairly compensates the writers, producers, artists, and creators of this music.

—Yahoo!, November 6, 2014

I DIDN'T THINK that it would be shocking to anyone [not to release *1989* on Spotify]. With as many ways as artists are personalizing their musical distribution, it didn't occur to me that this would be anything that anyone would talk about. But I could never have expected so many text messages, emails and phone calls from other artists, writers and producers saying thank you.

—*Hollywood Reporter*, December 17, 2014

I'M SURE YOU are aware that Apple Music will be offering a free 3 month trial to anyone who signs up for the service. I'm not sure you know that Apple Music will not be paying writers, producers, or artists for those three months. I find it to be shocking, disappointing, and completely unlike this historically progressive and generous company.

—letter to Apple Music, June 21, 2015

THE CONTRACTS [WITH Apple Music] had just gone out to my friends, and one of them sent me a screenshot of one of them. I read the term "zero percent compensation to rights holders." Sometimes I'll wake up in the middle of the night and I'll write a song and I can't sleep until I finish it, and it was like that with the letter [to Apple Music].

—*Vanity Fair*, August 11, 2015

> **EDITORIAL NOTE:** The "rights holders" mentioned by Swift are typically the songwriters who wrote the song and the person or company that owns the recording. Both earn small payments when a song is streamed. By offering "zero percent compensation" to rights holders, Apple Music was saying they weren't going to pay them anything for songs streamed during a new user's free trial. Because of Swift's public letter to Apple Music, they agreed to change course and pay artists for this period of time.

I'VE BEEN VERY optimistic and enthusiastic about the state of the music industry, and thankfully so have my fans. And they proved that they're ready and willing to invest in music and pay their hard-earned money to buy music. And I think it made an incredible statement, especially in this time in music.

—*Good Morning America*, **November 11, 2014**

IF YOU LOOK at ... how people used to gather around a record player to listen to music, it was such a social event. And now these days we have, I think, a responsibility to try and turn music back into a social event. . . . I think it's really kind of exciting that we have so many outlets now to make a song back into something that people not only listen to, but kind of assign to their memories and talk about with their friends.

—*The Kyle & Jackie O Show*, April 29, 2019

MY GENERATION WAS raised being able to flip channels if we got bored, and we read the last page of the book when we got impatient. We want to be caught off guard, delighted, left in awe. I hope the next generation's artists will continue to think of inventive ways of keeping their audiences on their toes, as challenging as that might be.

—*Wall Street Journal*, July 7, 2014

IT'S REALLY IMPORTANT to me to see eye to eye with a label regarding the future of our industry. I feel so motivated by new opportunities created by the streaming world and the ever changing landscape of our industry . . . I also feel strongly that streaming was founded on and continues to thrive based on the magic created by artists, writers, and producers.

—**Instagram post, November 19, 2018**

AS PART OF my new contract with Universal Music Group, I asked that any sale of their Spotify shares result in a distribution of money to their artists, **non-recoupable**. . . . I see this as a sign that we are headed towards positive change for creators—a goal I'm never going to stop trying to help achieve.

—**Instagram post, November 19, 2018**

NON-RECOUPABLE (adj): not able to regain

EDITORIAL NOTE: In recording contracts, an artist might get an upfront payment, called an advance, when they sign a deal with a recording label. Most advances are recoupable, meaning the artist has to pay the label back with the money they earn from music sales. Swift made Universal agree that if they sold any of their Spotify shares, they would give some of the money to artists and not require it to be paid back.

I SPENT 10 years of my life trying **rigorously** to purchase my masters outright and was then denied that opportunity.... God, I would have paid so much for them! Anything to own my work that was an actual sale option, but it wasn't given to me.

—on the sale of her master recordings to Scooter Braun,
***Billboard*, December 11, 2019**

RIGOROUSLY (adv): strictly, intensely

EDITORIAL NOTE: The master recording of a song is the original recording of it. Most artists do not own their own master recordings, even if they do hold a copyright for writing the song. The recording label owns the master until they decide to sell it to someone else.

[THE RE-RECORDING PROCESS is] going to be fun, because it'll feel like regaining a freedom and taking back what's mine. When I created [these songs], I didn't know what they would grow up to be. Going back in and knowing that it meant something to people is actually a really beautiful way to celebrate what the fans have done for my music.

—*Billboard*, December 11, 2019

Call It What You Want: Celebrity and Controversy

YOU CAN'T BELIEVE too much of your positive hype, and you can't believe too much of your negative press—you live somewhere in between.

—*Vanity Fair*, August 11, 2015

I JUST FEEL like you have to have a **perception** change when your life shifts into the gear of everybody knows who you are. You have to focus on thinking about it in the perspective of: I'm gonna go shopping right now. It's not gonna take the amount of time that it used to take before people knew who I was. It's gonna take double. And I'm cool with that, because this is what I wanted and I'm one of the lucky people who actually got what they wanted in life.

—*The Hot Desk*, May 2009

PERCEPTION (noun): a way of understanding something

PLAYING STADIUMS . . . walking down the street
. . . I'd choose playing stadiums. It's a trade-off.
There's no way to travel two roads at once. You
pick one. And if you don't like the road you're
on, you change direction. You don't sit there and
go, "Oh, I wish I could have all the good things in
the world and none of the bad things." It doesn't
work like that.

—*NME*, October 9, 2015

IF I KNOW I can't deal with talking to people that
day, I just don't go out. I just have to wake up in
the morning and say, How am I feeling today?
If someone asks for a picture, am I gonna feel
imposed upon today because I'm dealing with my
own stuff? Am I gonna take my own stuff out on
some innocent 14-year-old today and be in a bad
mood? Okay, maybe not . . . Maybe I won't leave
the house.

—*Esquire*, October 20, 2014

I DON'T KNOW if I'll have kids. It's impossible not to picture certain scenarios and how you would try to convince them that they have a normal life when, inevitably, there will be strange men pointing giant cameras at them from the time they are babies.

—*InStyle*, November 2014

I'M REALISTIC ABOUT the fact that millions of people don't have time in their day to maintain a complex profile of who I am. They're busy with their work and their kids and their husband or their boyfriend and their friends. They only have time to come up with about two or three adjectives to describe people in the public eye. And that's okay. As long as those three adjectives aren't *train wreck, mess, terrible.*

—*Esquire*, October 20, 2014

THERE IS A little bit of an imbalance where all these people know aspects of your personality. They feel they know you, they know your cats' names and all this stuff. But at the same time, you're meeting them for the first time.

—**Beats 1, December 13, 2015**

I DO NOT give an edited version of myself to my friends. [And] anytime I read one of those tabloid articles that says, "A source close to Swift says," it's always incorrect. None of my friends are talking, and they know *everything*.

—*Vanity Fair*, **August 11, 2015**

YOU KNOW WHAT I've found works even better than an NDA? Looking someone in the eye and saying, "Please don't tell anyone about this."

—*Rolling Stone*, **September 8, 2014**

EDITORIAL NOTE: An NDA is a nondisclosure agreement. It's a contract in which someone agrees not to disclose, or tell, certain information to anyone.

THERE ARE A lot of really easy ways to **dispel** rumors. If they say you are pregnant, all you have to do is continue to not be pregnant and not have a baby. If the rumor is that you have fake friendships, all you have to do is continue to be there for each other. And when we're all friends in fifteen years and raising our kids together, maybe somebody will look back and go, "That was kind of ridiculous what we said about Taylor and her friends."

—*Vogue*, April 14, 2016

DISPEL (verb): get rid of

I LOOK AT some of my best friends who are doing the most amazing work, creating the most amazing things, setting the best example for women and girls—and because of that they're the biggest targets.

There's a really dark side of humanity and a very dark corner of the internet, and they know that the most value will be if they can take down someone who is really doing good things.

—the *Sun*, October 27, 2014

I THINK THE reason a lot of celebrities feel insecure and want to stop eating altogether is because they see so many pictures of themselves on a daily basis. It's unhealthy how many times you see your own image—it's just constant. When you see something enough, you're going to tear it down to the point where some days you feel like you're not even pretty.

—*Glamour*, July 1, 2009

I DON'T LIKE seeing slide shows of guys I've apparently dated. I don't like giving comedians the opportunity to make jokes about me at awards shows. I don't like it when headlines read "Careful, Bro, She'll Write a Song About You," because it **trivializes** my work. And most of all, I don't like how all these factors add up to build the pressure so high in a new relationship that it gets snuffed out before it even has a chance to start.

—*Rolling Stone*, September 8, 2014

TRIVIALIZES (verb): makes something seem unimportant or silly

I JUST DECIDED I wasn't willing to provide them that kind of entertainment anymore. I wasn't going to go out on dates and have them be allowed to take pictures and say whatever they wanted about our body language. I wasn't going to sit next to somebody and flirt with them for five minutes, because I know the next day he'll be rumored to be my boyfriend. I just kind of took the narrative back.

—*Vogue*, **February 13, 2015**

WHEN YOU SAY a relationship is public, that means I'm going to see him do what he loves, we're showing up for each other, other people are there and we don't care. The opposite of that is you have to go to an extreme amount of effort to make sure no one knows that you're seeing someone.

—*Time*, **December 6, 2023**

THEY CAN SAY whatever they want about my personal life because I know what my personal life is, and it involves a lot of TV and cats and girlfriends. But I don't like it when they start to make cheap shots at my songwriting. Because there's no joke to be made there.

—*Guardian*, August 23, 2014

I THINK THAT as a songwriter you're supposed to stay open, and you're supposed to stay vulnerable, and you're supposed to feel pain and feel it intensely. As a celebrity, you're kind of encouraged to put up these emotional walls and block out all the voices saying terrible things about you and to you. And so they're mixed messages, and I'm trying to kind of like walk a tightrope in between the two.

—BBC Radio 1, October 9, 2014

WHEN YOU PUT out one song or you're in one movie, what you don't realize is that no matter what, you're a role model, whether you choose to embrace it or whether you choose to ignore it. And I just choose to embrace it because I feel like it's the biggest honor in the world when a mom comes up to me and says, "My eight-year-old daughter listens to your music, and I think that it's so great that she looks up to you."

—*The Ellen DeGeneres Show*, **November 11, 2008**

I THINK ABOUT what—if I'm lucky enough to have grandkids someday—what they would say if they went back and looked back at pictures and videos and things like that. And I'm sure they'd laugh at me and, like, make fun of my awkwardness and things like that, but I would never want to embarrass them. And it's interesting because it's like this whole role model question. Like, are you a role model? Do you think about the little kids in the front row when you're doing all the things you're doing in your life? I think that's an unnecessary pressure to put on yourself, but it's easier when you make it about your own life, your own **legacy**, when you kind of bring it in-house and you're like, "What if I have a five-year-old someday?"

—"Taylor Swift 1989," October 27, 2014

LEGACY (noun): what someone leaves behind, what people remember of them

I KNEW OTHER people can make partying look cute and edgy but, if I did, people were going to twist it into this tragic America's-sweetheart-goes-off-the-rails-and-loses-her-mind thing. So I just made sure that that could never be written about me, and I don't feel like I missed out.

—British *Vogue*, November 2014

I FOUGHT THE idea of having security for a very long time, because I really value normalcy.... I like to be able to take a drive by myself. Haven't done that in six years.... The sheer number of men we have in a file who have showed up at my house, showed up at my mom's house, threatened to either kill me, kidnap me, or marry me. This is the strange and sad part of my life that I try not to think about. I try to be lighthearted about it, because I don't ever want to be scared.... And when I have security, I don't have to be scared.

—*Esquire*, October 20, 2014

EDITORIAL NOTE: Many celebrities who have received threats of violence hire security details (bodyguards) to protect them while they're out in public and even at home.

SOMETHING THAT SCARES me a little bit is how valuable it would be to find something that I've done wrong, or to find something that is problematic about me. You know, I do have moments where I get really scared, like, who's trying to take pictures in my hotel room window? You live your life with the blinds drawn, like, in every room you go into. And that's the part that kind of gets to me sometimes, is, like, every day, like right now, there's someone in TMZ trying to dig through my trash and figure out what I did wrong.

—Beats 1, December 13, 2015

EDITORIAL NOTE: TMZ is a celebrity news outlet known for using questionable methods for getting a story, such as buying photos and videos from paparazzi.

A COUPLE OF years ago, someone called me a snake on social media, and it caught on. And then a lot of people were calling me a lot of things on social media. And I went through some really low times for a while because of it. I went through some times when I didn't know if I was gonna get to do this anymore. And I guess the snakes [onstage], I wanted to send a message to you guys that if someone uses name-calling to bully you on social media, and even if a lot of people jump on board with it, that doesn't have to defeat you. It can strengthen you instead.

—*Reputation* Stadium Tour, Glendale, Arizona,
May 8, 2018

WHEN THIS ALBUM comes out, gossip blogs will scour the lyrics for the men they can **attribute** to each song, as if the inspiration for music is as simple and basic as a **paternity test**. There will be slideshows of photos backing up each incorrect theory, because it's 2017 and if you didn't see a picture of it, it couldn't have happened right? . . .

There will be no further explanation.

There will just be reputation.

—*Reputation* magazine, November 10, 2017

ATTRIBUTE (verb): assign to

PATERNITY TEST (noun): a medical test that determines if a person is the father of a particular child

[YOUR REPUTATION] IS only real if it stops you from getting to know someone where you feel like you can connect with them in a really real way.

—**Taylor Swift NOW secret show, June 28, 2018**

I WAS PRETTY proud of coining the term "There will be no explanation. There will just be reputation." . . . I didn't try to explain the album because I didn't feel that I owed that to anyone. There was a lot that happened over a couple of years that made me feel really, really terrible. And I didn't feel like expressing that to them. I didn't feel like talking about it. I just felt like making music, then going out on the road and doing a stadium tour and doing everything I could for my fans.

—**Beats 1, May 1, 2019**

THE WHOLE TIME that I was writing an album
[*Reputation*] based on all the facets of a
reputation and how it affects you, what it actually
means to you, I was surrounded by friends and
family and loved ones who never loved me less
based on the **fluctuations** of public opinion.

—2018 American Music Awards, October 9, 2018

FLUCTUATIONS (noun): changes and shifts

Part III

THE WISDOM OF TAYLOR SWIFT

Speak Now:

Finding a Political Voice

I DON'T REALLY think about things as guys versus girls. I never have. I was raised by parents who brought me up to think if you work as hard as guys, you can go far in life.

—*Daily Beast*, October 22, 2012

EDITORIAL NOTE: Swift was twenty-two years old when she made this statement. As she got older and had more experience in her profession, her ideas changed, as is clear from the quotations related to feminism later in this section.

I WROTE A song called "Mean" about a critic who hated me. I put it out, and all of a sudden, it became an anthem against bullies in schools, which is a refreshing and new take on it. When people say things about me empowering women, that's an amazing compliment. It's not necessarily what I thought I was doing, because I write songs about what I feel. I think there's strength when you're baring your emotions.

—*Daily Beast*, October 22, 2012

I HAVE A lot to learn about politics and feminism—all these huge incredible concepts. I want to end up being really educated about all these big topics that everyone talks about, but, I mean, it's like baby steps, you know? And until I really form an opinion that I feel is educated, I just don't know if I can talk about it.

—*Elle* **Canada, November 19, 2012**

IN THE PAST I've been reluctant to publicly voice my political opinions, but due to several events in my life and in the world in the past two years, I feel very differently about that now. I always have and always will cast my vote based on which candidate will protect and fight for the human rights I believe we all deserve in this country. I believe in the fight for LGBTQ rights, and that any form of discrimination based on sexual orientation or gender is WRONG. I believe that the systemic racism we still see in this country towards people of color is terrifying, sickening and **prevalent**.

—Instagram post, October 7, 2018

PREVALENT (adj): common or widespread

EDITORIAL NOTE: In 2018, Swift finally broke her political silence, posting on Instagram in support of the Democratic candidate, Phil Bredesen, who was running for Senate in Swift's home state of Tennessee. The Republican candidate, Marsha Blackburn, ended up beating Bredesen in the election, but this marked the beginning of Swift using her platform for political activism.

INVOKING RACISM AND provoking fear through thinly veiled messaging is not what I want from our leaders, and I realized that it actually is my responsibility to use my influence against that disgusting rhetoric. I'm going to do more to help. We have a big race coming up next year.

—*Elle*, **March 6, 2019**

INVOKING (verb): calling forth as explanation

IT'S VERY BRAVE to be vulnerable about your feelings in any sense, in any situation. But it's even more brave to be honest about your feelings and who you love when you know that that might be met with adversity from society. So, this [Pride Month] and every month, I want to send out my love and respect to everybody who has been brave enough to be honest about how they feel, to live their lives as they are, as they feel they should be, as they identify. And this is a month where I think we need to celebrate how far we've come. We also need to acknowledge how far we still have left to go.

—*Reputation* **Stadium Tour, Chicago, Illinois,
June 2, 2018**

I THINK I was probably 15 the first time I was asked about [feminism]. And so I would just say, "I don't talk about politics. I don't really understand that stuff yet, so I guess I'm just gonna say I'm not [a feminist]." And I wish that when I was younger I would have known that it's simply hoping for gender equality.

—**"Taylor Swift 1989," October 27, 2014**

I THINK THAT when I used to say, "Oh, feminism's not really on my radar," it was because when I was just seen as a kid, I wasn't as threatening. I didn't see myself being held back until I was a woman.

—*Maxim*, May 11, 2015

I DON'T FEEL great when I am fed messages, and when I was fed messages as a young girl, that it's more important to be edgy and sexy and cool than anything else. I don't think that those are the right messages to feed girls.... My life doesn't **gravitate** towards being edgy, sexy, or cool.... I am imaginative, I am smart, and I'm hardworking. And those things are not necessarily prioritized in pop culture.

—*CBS This Morning*, October 29, 2014

I JUST STRUGGLE to find a woman in music who hasn't been completely picked apart by the media, or **scrutinized** and criticized for aging, or criticized for fighting aging. It just seems to be much more difficult to be a woman in music and to grow older. I just really hope that I will choose to do it as gracefully as possible.

—*Time*, November 13, 2014

SCRUTINIZED (verb): looked at very closely, analyzed

ONE THING THAT I do believe as a feminist is that, in order for us to have gender equality, we have to stop making it a girl fight and we have to stop being so interested in seeing girls try to tear each other down. It has to be more about cheering each other on as women.

—*Tout le monde en parle*, September 28, 2014

IF A GUY shares his experience in writing, he's brave. If a woman shares her experience in writing, she's oversharing and she's overemotional. Or she might be crazy. Or, "Watch out, she'll write a song about you!" That joke is so old. And it's coming from a place of such sexism.

—"Barbara Walters Presents: The 10 Most Fascinating People of 2014," December 15, 2014

IN 2013, I met a DJ from a prominent country radio station in one of my pre-show meet and greets. When we were posing for the photo, he stuck his hand up my dress and grabbed onto my ass cheek. I squirmed and lurched sideways to get away from him, but he wouldn't let go. At the time, I was headlining a major arena tour and there were a number of people in the room that saw this *plus* a photo of it happening. I figured that if he would be brazen enough to assault me under these risky circumstances and high stakes, imagine what he might do to a vulnerable, young artist if given the chance.

—*Time*, December 6, 2017

WHEN I TESTIFIED, I had already been in court all week and had to watch this man's attorney bully, badger and harass my team including my mother over **inane** details and ridiculous **minutiae**, accusing them, and me, of lying. . . . I was angry. In that moment, I decided to forego any courtroom formalities and just answer the questions the way it happened. . . . I'm told it was the most amount of times the word "ass" has ever been said in Colorado Federal Court.

—*Time*, December 6, 2017

INANE (adj): pointless and insignificant

MINUTIAE (noun): tiny details

WHEN THE JURY found in my favor, the man who sexually assaulted me was court-ordered to give me a symbolic $1. To this day he has not paid me that dollar, and I think that act of defiance is symbolic in itself.

—*Time*, December 6, 2017

EDITORIAL NOTE: Swift only asked for $1 because she wanted to send a message that the case wasn't about money, but rather about standing up for others who are groped and lack the resources to take legal action. The DJ in question claimed he mailed Swift a $1 coin just before this *Time* interview was published.

THIS DAY A year ago was the day that the jury sided in my favor and said that they believed me. I guess I just think about all the people that weren't believed and the people who haven't been believed, or the people who are afraid to speak up because they think they won't be believed. And I just wanted to say I'm sorry to anyone who ever wasn't believed, because I don't know what turn my life would've taken if somebody—if people didn't believe me when I said that something had happened to me. And so I guess I just wanted to say that we have so, so, so much further to go, and I'm so grateful to you guys for being there for me during what was a really, really horrible part of my life.

—*Reputation* **Stadium Tour, Tampa, Florida,**
August 14, 2018

THERE IS A great deal of blame placed on the victims in cases of sexual harassment and assault.... My advice is that you not blame yourself and do not accept the blame others will try to place on you. You should not be blamed for waiting 15 minutes or 15 days or 15 years to report sexual assault or harassment, or for the outcome of what happens to a person after [they make] the choice to sexually harass or assault you.

—*Time*, December 6, 2017

Shake It Off:

And Other

Life Lessons

WITH THE SONG "Shake It Off," I really wanted to kind of take back the narrative, and have more of a sense of humor about people who kind of get under my skin—and *not let* them get under my skin. There's a song that I wrote a couple years ago called "Mean," where I addressed the same issue but I addressed it very differently. I said, "Why you gotta be so mean?" from kind of a victimized perspective, which is how we all approach bullying or gossip when it happens to us for the first time. But in the last few years I've gotten better at just kind of laughing off things that absolutely have no bearing on my real life.

—*All Things Considered*, October 31, 2014

YOU CAN GET everything you want in life without ever feeling like you fit in. You know, selling millions of records doesn't make me feel cool. Like, it makes me feel proud, and like I have a lot of people on my side and I've worked really hard, but, you know, I don't think it's the most important thing in life to fit in. I think it's the most important thing in life to dance to the beat of your own drum and to look like you're having more fun than the people who look cool.

—behind the scenes of the "Shake It Off" music video,
September 11, 2014

I FEEL LIKE dancing is sort of a metaphor for the way you live your life. You know how you're at a house party and there's a group of people over there just talking and rolling their eyes at everyone dancing? And you know which group is having more fun.

—*Guardian*, August 23, 2014

WHEN SOMEBODY CRITICIZES you or says something behind your back, those words that they said about you, it's like you feel like those words are written all over your face, all over you. And then those words start to become echoes in your own mind. And then there's a real risk that those words could become a part of how you see yourself. The moment that you realize that you are not the opinion of somebody who doesn't know you or care about you, that moment when you realize that is like you're clean.

—*The* 1989 *World Tour Live*, December 20, 2015

DESPITE OUR NEED to simplify and generalize absolutely everyone and everything in this life, humans are **intrinsically** impossible to simplify. We are never just good or just bad. We are mosaics of our worst selves and our best selves, our deepest secrets and our favorite stories to tell at a dinner party.

—*Reputation* magazine, November 10, 2017

INTRINSICALLY (adj): naturally, automatically

WHEN I WAS growing up and I was in school, I hated my hair. I have really curly hair. . . . Everybody had straight hair, and I wanted straight hair so bad. And I always tried to straighten it, and I spent, like, hours in the morning trying. And then I woke up one day and I realized that just because something is different than everybody else doesn't make it bad.

—behind the scenes of *Seventeen* cover shoot, May 5, 2008

IF YOU THINK about human nature, our favorite pair of shoes is the one we bought yesterday. Our favorite thing is the newest thing that we have. And if you think about the thing that we've seen the most and for the longest period of time, [it's] our reflection in the mirror, so obviously that's gonna be our least favorite thing.

—*Loose Women*, **February 18, 2009**

ONE OF MY best friends is this pageant queen. . . . Everybody wants to be her, all the guys want to date her. And I wrote ["Tied Together with a Smile"] the day that I found out she had an eating disorder. You know, it's kind of a halting point in your life when you realize that something that you thought was so strong, you find out that it isn't strong at all.

—**"Tied Together with a Smile" commentary,**
Taylor Swift **(Big Machine Radio Release Special),**
December 13, 2018

I LEARNED TO stop hating every ounce of fat on my body. I worked hard to retrain my brain that a little extra weight means curves, shinier hair, and more energy. I think a lot of us push the boundaries of dieting, but taking it too far can be really dangerous. There is no quick fix. I work on accepting my body every day.

—*Elle*, **March 6, 2019**

THE PEOPLE WHO strike me as beautiful are the people who have their own thing going on. . . . Unique and different is the next generation of beautiful. You don't have to be the same as everybody else. In fact, I don't think you should.

—**behind the scenes of CoverGirl commercial shoot, April 22, 2010**

I THINK IT'S healthy for your self-esteem to need less internet praise to appease it, especially when three comments down you could unwittingly see someone telling you that you look like a weasel that got hit by a truck and stitched back together by a drunk **taxidermist**. An actual comment I received once.

—*Elle*, March 6, 2019

TAXIDERMIST (noun): a person who preserves dead animals by preparing and stuffing them, often in life-like poses, so the animals can be displayed or studied

EDITORIAL NOTE: Swift has commenting turned off on her social media accounts as a way to avoid both seeing negative comments and needing to see positive ones.

WORDS CAN BREAK someone into a million pieces, but they can also put them back together. I hope you use yours for good, because the only words you'll regret more than the ones left unsaid are the ones you use to intentionally hurt someone.

—Speak Now liner notes, October 25, 2010

APOLOGIZING WHEN YOU have hurt someone who really matters to you takes nothing away from you. Even if it was unintentional, it's so easy to just apologize and move on. Try not to say "I'm sorry, but . . ." and make excuses for yourself. Learn how to make a sincere apology, and you can avoid breaking down the trust in your friendships and relationships.

—Elle, March 6, 2019

"BAD BLOOD" IS a song that I wrote about a new kind of heartbreak that I experienced recently, which was when someone that I desperately wanted to be my friend and thought was my friend ended up really making it very obvious that she wasn't. . . . This song was kind of the first time I ever really stood up for myself in that relationship because she was always the bolder one and the louder one. And, like, I think it's important to stand up for yourself, and if you can only really come up with the courage to do it in song form, then that's how you should do it.

—"Bad Blood" commentary, *1989* (Big Machine Radio Release Special), December 13, 2018

BEING SWEET TO everyone all the time can get you into a lot of trouble. While it may be born from having been raised to be a polite young lady, this can contribute to some of your life's worst regrets if someone takes advantage of this trait in you. Grow a backbone, trust your gut, and know when to strike back. Be like a snake—only bite if someone steps on you.

—*Elle*, March 6, 2019

> **EDITORIAL NOTE:** Following the release of *Reputation*,
> Swift continued to use snake imagery, which was present in
> the album's song lyrics, music videos, and concert set design,
> as a way to reclaim the narrative about her being called a snake
> on social media. A snake makes an appearance in the music
> video for the first single off of *Lover* before bursting into pastel
> butterflies. Fans believe this is a symbol of her "shedding her
> skin" and moving on from the snake image.

THERE IS A tendency to block out negative
things because they really hurt. But if I stop
feeling pain, then I'm afraid that I'll stop feeling
immense excitement and epic celebration and
happiness, which, I can't stop feeling those
things. So, I feel everything. And I think that
keeps me who I am.

—*USA Today* **audio interview, October 27, 2010**

IT'S ALL ABOUT walking a tightrope between not
being so fragile and breakable that they can level
you with one blow and being raw enough to feel it
and write about it when you feel it.

—*Esquire*, **October 20, 2014**

I TRY TO encourage my fans that they don't have to feel confident every day, they don't have to feel happy every day, they don't have to feel pretty every day, they don't have to feel wanted every day, that they shouldn't put added extra pressure on themselves to feel happy when they're not, you know? I think being honest with yourself emotionally is really important.

—"Taylor Swift 1989," October 27, 2014

I FEEL LIKE we're sent so many messages every day that there's, like, a better version of us on a social media app with, like, better apps and a better vacation spot. But, like, you're the only one of you. That's it. There's just you.

—Apple Music video, April 26, 2019

LIFE CAN BE beautiful and **spontaneous** and
surprising and romantic and magical without
you having some love affair happening. And you
can replace all of those feelings you used to have
when you were **enamored** with someone with
being enamored with your friends and enamored
with learning new things and challenging
yourself and living your life on your own terms.

—*Q*, October 28, 2014

SPONTANEOUS (adj): sudden, unexpected

ENAMORED (adj): feeling love and affection toward

WHEN YOUR NUMBER-ONE priority is getting a boyfriend, you're more inclined to see a beautiful girl and think, "Oh, she's gonna get that hot guy I wish I was dating." But when you're not boyfriend-shopping, you're able to step back and see other girls who are killing it and think, "God, I want to be around her."

—*Rolling Stone*, September 8, 2014

IT'S SO MUCH easier to like people, and to let people in, to trust them until they prove that you should do otherwise. The alternative is being an iceberg.

—the *Australian*, March 5, 2009

"LOOK WHAT YOU Made Me Do," it actually started with just, like, a poem that I wrote about my feelings. And it's basically about, like, realizing that you couldn't trust certain people but realizing you appreciate the people you can trust, realizing that you can't just let everyone in, but the ones you can let in you need to cherish.

—*Reputation* Secret Session, October 2017

I JUDGE PEOPLE based on their moral code; I think someone is nothing without a moral code. I don't care if you're talented or celebrated or successful or rich or popular, if you have no moral code. If you will betray your friend, if you will talk about them badly behind their back, if you will try to humiliate them or talk down to them, I have no interest in having a person like that in my life.

—*Vanity Fair*, August 11, 2015

A GENERAL RULE is that if you do the right thing, a lot of times that pans out in a business sense. If you start out trying to do things in a business sense, a lot of times it falls flat on its face.

—*60 Minutes*, November 20, 2011

WHEN OTHER KIDS were watching normal shows, I'd watch *Behind the Music*. And I would see these bands that were doing so well, and I'd wonder what went wrong. I thought about this a lot. And what I established in my brain was that a lack of self-awareness was always the downfall. That was always the **catalyst** for the loss of **relevance** and the loss of ambition and the loss of great art. So self-awareness has been such a huge part of what I try to achieve on a daily basis.

—*GQ*, October 15, 2015

> CATALYST (noun): an event that starts a sequence of following events

RELEVANCE (noun): importance to the matter at hand

EDITORIAL NOTE: *Behind the Music* was a TV show that premiered in the late 1990s. Each episode featured one artist or band and dove into their background, successes, and difficulties.

I TRY TO be really aware of the fact that, like, something is golden and magical and special—for a time. And if you drag it out, I never want people to be like, "Will she just go away now?" Because it happens!

—Beats 1, December 13, 2015

I GET REALLY, really excited and happy about the same things that I used to get excited and happy about, like the small things like going to the grocery store and like hanging out with friends and all that. I think if you stay on a level where you can be happy about little things as well as the crazy, big things that are going on in your life, it keeps it balanced.

—rehearsals for the 52nd Annual Grammy Awards,
January 31, 2010

BOTH OF MY parents have had cancer, and my mom is now fighting her battle with it again. It's taught me that there are real problems and then there's everything else. My mom's cancer is a real problem. I used to be so anxious about daily ups and downs. I give all of my worry, stress, and prayers to real problems now.

—*Elle*, March 6, 2019

OVER THE YEARS, I've learned I don't have the time or **bandwidth** to get pressed about things that don't matter. Yes, if I go out to dinner, there's going to be a whole chaotic situation outside the restaurant. But I still want to go to dinner with my friends. Life is short. Have adventures. Me locking myself away in my house for a lot of years—I'll never get that time back. I'm more trusting now than I was six years ago.

—Time, December 6, 2023

BANDWIDTH (noun): the mental or emotional energy needed to do something

---

DURING THE FIRST few years of your career, the only thing anyone says to you is "Enjoy this. Just enjoy this." That's all they ever tell you. And I finally know how to do that.

—GQ, October 15, 2015

THE THING ABOUT doing what you love is you never know if it's gonna happen, and you never know if you're gonna get to do it one more day. But the fact that you're doing it right now, or trying to do it, or working towards it, it's like stepping stones. . . . If you really love it, the stepping stones working towards it are just as rewarding as getting to do it and ending up with that as your job.

—*VH1 Storytellers*, November 11, 2012

I'M ALSO THANKFUL that when I go to sleep at night I get to know that I've been myself that day. And I've been myself all the days before that.

—"NBC's People of the Year," November 26, 2009

ONE THING I'VE learned, and possibly the only advice I have to give, is to not be that person giving out **unsolicited** advice based on your own personal experience. I've always had a lot of older people giving me advice because I'm young, and in the end, it all comes down to who you want to be remembered as. Just be that.

—*Billboard*, May 25, 2013

UNSOLICITED (adj): not asked for

Milestones

1989

- Taylor Alison Swift is born on December 13, 1989, in Reading, Pennsylvania, to Scott and Andrea Swift. She spends her early years on a Christmas tree farm owned by her parents in Wyomissing, Pennsylvania, although her dad also works as a stockbroker for Merrill Lynch.

2002

- Swift performs the national anthem at a Philadelphia 76ers game.

2003

- Swift enters into a development deal with RCA Records. By the end of the year, the label decides to wait until she is eighteen to consider putting out a record with her. Swift chooses to walk away from RCA instead of waiting for their decision.

- Swift models for an Abercrombie & Fitch Rising Stars campaign.

2004

- Swift's song "The Outside" is included on the compilation CD *Maybelline New York Presents Chicks with Attitude*.

- Scott Swift transfers to the Nashville office of Merrill Lynch to get Taylor closer to Nashville's Music Row. The family lives in Hendersonville, Tennessee, outside Nashville.

- Swift starts her freshman year at Hendersonville High School and meets her longtime friend Abigail Anderson, who is later featured in the song "Fifteen."

- Swift performs at The Bluebird Cafe in Nashville and Scott Borchetta, a country music veteran working at Universal Music Group Nashville, offers to sign Swift to his new label.

2005

- Swift signs a publishing deal with Sony/ATV Music Publishing. She is the youngest songwriter ever brought on by the publishing house.

- Borchetta creates Big Machine Records and signs Swift to the label.

2006

- Swift finishes her sophomore year (which also happens to be her last year) at Hendersonville High School. After leaving Hendersonville High she is homeschooled to give her time to focus on her music and career.

- Swift's first single, "Tim McGraw," is released. Swift had written the song in class as she thought of her boyfriend, who would be moving away to college in the fall. She cowrote the song with Liz Rose, a frequent collaborator who often describes herself as Swift's "editor." The single peaks at number six on the *Billboard* Hot Country Songs chart—likely due, in part, to the big name in its title.

- *Taylor Swift* is released. Swift cowrote many of the songs on the album with Rose while Swift was still a full-time student in high school. After trying out a number of more seasoned producers, Swift also brought on Nathan Chapman, her longtime demo partner and a first-time producer, to produce all but one of the tracks on the album. Swift spends months promoting the album on a cross-country radio tour and is rewarded when the album peaks at number five on the *Billboard* 200 chart and is eventually certified seven times platinum by the Recording Industry Association of America (RIAA). "Teardrops on My Guitar," "Our Song," and "Picture to Burn" are several notable singles released from the album, in addition to lead single "Tim McGraw."

- Swift opens for Rascal Flatts on their *Me and My Gang* Tour.

2007

- Along with Kellie Pickler and Jack Ingram, Swift opens for Brad Paisley on his Bonfires & Amplifiers Tour.

- Swift is nominated for Top New Female Vocalist at the 42nd Annual Academy of Country Music Awards (ACM Awards). She doesn't win, but she does meet Tim McGraw for the first time during her live performance of "Tim McGraw."

- Swift opens for Tim McGraw and Faith Hill on select dates of their Soul2Soul II Tour.

- "Our Song" is released as a single, becoming Swift's first number one on the *Billboard* Hot Country Songs chart.

- Swift celebrates her favorite holiday on the EP *Sounds of the Season: The Taylor Swift Holiday Collection.*

- Swift wins the Horizon Award (given to promising new artists) at the 2007 Country Music Association Awards (CMA Awards).

2008

- This year, Swift does win Top New Female Vocalist at the ACM Awards.

- Swift dates Joe Jonas, who later breaks up with her over a twenty-seven-second phone call that she describes on *The Ellen DeGeneres Show.* Jonas is one of the few boyfriends Swift admits to dating; she later adopts a tight-lipped policy when it comes to her relationships.

- Swift befriends Selena Gomez while they are both dating Jonas brothers. The friendship between the two (not to mention their careers) flourishes after their breakups.

- Swift graduates from high school.

- Swift's *Beautiful Eyes* EP is released in an exclusive deal with Walmart.

- "Love Story," written about a boy Swift liked but her parents didn't approve of, is released as the lead single from *Fearless.* "Love Story" becomes one of Swift's first crossover hits, charting well on the pop as well as the country charts. It is also one of her first true international successes, reaching number one on the Canadian and Australian music charts.

- *Fearless*, Swift's second album, is released. Swift continues her working relationship with Rose and Chapman for her second album while bringing on new collaborators like Colbie Caillat and John Rich. She also coproduces all the songs on the album herself for the first time. Some of Swift's (arguably) most iconic songs, including "Love Story," "You Belong with Me," and "Fifteen," are released as singles from the album. *Fearless*, like "Love Story," is a huge crossover success, reaching number one on the *Billboard* 200 chart and becoming the best-selling album of 2009. It is ranked fourth on the Greatest of All Time *Billboard* 200 Albums chart.

- Swift wins Favorite Female Artist—Country at the American Music Awards (AMAs).

2009

- Swift appears on *CSI*, one of her favorite TV shows—fulfilling her dream of playing a character who is murdered on the show.

- Swift launches her first solo concert tour in support of *Fearless*. The sold-out tour starts in Evansville, Indiana, and goes to Asia, Australia, and Europe.

- Swift has a small role playing herself in *Hannah Montana: The Movie*. She also contributes a song, "Crazier," to the soundtrack.

- Swift wins the Crystal Milestone Award at the 44th Annual ACM Awards to recognize her success in bringing young and international fans to country music. She also wins Album of the Year for *Fearless*.

- Swift opens for Keith Urban on select dates of his Escape Together World Tour.

- Swift wins the award for Best Female Video for "You Belong with Me" at the 2009 MTV Video Music Awards (VMAs). Kanye West, in an instantly infamous moment, goes onstage to interrupt her acceptance speech and insist that Beyoncé should have won the award instead. Swift receives an outpouring of support, including from Beyoncé and President Barack Obama, but the incident introduces a long-standing rift between Swift and West.

- *Fearless Platinum Edition* is released after *Fearless* goes platinum. It includes new songs and a DVD of music videos and behind-the-scenes footage.

- Swift hosts and performs on *Saturday Night Live*, notably writing her own musical monologue, which pokes fun at her often boy-crazy lyrics.

- The 57th Annual BMI Country Awards names "Love Story" Song of the Year.

- Swift wins five awards at the CMA Awards, including Entertainer of the Year and Album of the Year (for *Fearless*).

- Swift wins five of the six AMAs she is nominated for, including Artist of the Year and Favorite Country Album for *Fearless*.

- Swift briefly dates John Mayer.

- Swift purchases her first home, moving out of her parents' house and into a $1.99 million condo in Nashville.

2010

- Swift wins her first Grammy (Best Female Country Vocal Performance for "White Horse") and becomes the youngest person to ever win Album of the Year (for *Fearless*). She also wins the Grammys for Best Country Album and Best Country Song (also for "White Horse").

- Swift has a small role in the ensemble romantic comedy *Valentine's Day*. On the set she meets and briefly dates Taylor Lautner, who stars as her love interest in the film.

- After prematurely leaking online, "Mine" is released as the first single from the upcoming album *Speak Now*. It reaches number two on the *Billboard* Hot Country Songs chart.

- *Speak Now* is released. There are no cowriters on the album, and it is to date Swift's only solo-written album. The album was initially called *Enchanted*, but Big Machine nudged Swift to change the name to move away from her more youthful fairy-tale inspirations. In addition to "Mine," "Back to December" and "Mean" are notable singles from the album. *Speak Now* debuts at number one on the *Billboard* 200 chart and sells 1 million copies within the first week of its release.

- Swift dates actor Jake Gyllenhaal. Their relationship and breakup reportedly inspire much of *Red* (although Swift never names names).

- At the 58th Annual BMI Country Music Awards, Swift becomes the youngest-ever winner of the Songwriter of the Year award. She also wins Song of the Year for "You Belong with Me."

- Swift wins the Favorite Female Artist—Country award at the AMAs.

2011

- Swift wins Entertainer of the Year, the top prize, at the 46th Annual ACM Awards.

- The *Speak Now* World Tour launches in Singapore. It goes on to become the highest-grossing solo tour of 2011.

- Swift purchases a home in Beverly Hills, California.

- Before the North American leg of the *Speak Now* tour, Swift opens up a rehearsal in Nashville to fans and uses the proceeds to help victims of tornadoes in the Southeast.

- Swift wins Top *Billboard* 200 Artist, Top Country Artist, and Top Country Album (for *Speak Now*) at the *Billboard* Music Awards (BBMAs).

- Swift wins the Jim Reeves International Award at an ACM Honors event. The award recognizes the efforts of musicians who bring international attention to country music.

- Swift is named *Billboard* Woman of the Year.

- Swift welcomes Meredith Grey, a Scottish fold cat named for the *Grey's Anatomy* protagonist, into her life.

- Swift wins her second Entertainer of the Year CMA Award.

- Swift wins for Favorite Country Female Artist, Favorite Country Album (for *Speak Now*), and Artist of the Year at the AMAs.

2012

- Swift wins two Grammys for the song "Mean."

- Swift turns in her first voiceover performance for the Dr. Seuss adaptation *The Lorax*.

- Michelle Obama presents Swift with the Big Help Award at the 25th Annual Nickelodeon Kids' Choice Awards in recognition of the singer's philanthropic efforts.

- Swift wins Entertainer of the Year at the ACM Awards for the second year in a row.

- Swift and Ed Sheeran become friends and collaborators after expressing a mutual interest in working together. Their first song together is "Everything Has Changed," reportedly written on a trampoline.

- "We Are Never Ever Getting Back Together," the lead single from *Red*, is released, becoming Swift's first song to reach number one on the *Billboard* Hot 100 chart.

- The Keds shoe brand partners with Swift to release a line of shoes and a series of videos that encourage bravery in young girls.

- *Red* is released. While her previous albums had all incorporated elements of pop as well as country, *Red* shows a marked step toward pop and away from her country influences. Swift collaborates for the first time with noted pop producers Max Martin and Shellback, who work on "22," "I Knew You Were Trouble," and "We Are Never Ever Getting Back Together." The album debuts at number one on the *Billboard* 200 chart and sells 1.208 million copies in its first week.

- Swift wins Favorite Female Artist—Country at the AMAs. She also premieres "I Knew You Were Trouble" at the ceremony.

- Swift dates One Direction member Harry Styles for several months. Fans will speculate that a number of the songs on *1989* are written about him.

2013

- Swift becomes a brand ambassador for Diet Coke.

- Swift launches the *Red* Tour in Omaha, Nebraska. The tour travels to Europe and Australia before wrapping in Asia and becoming the highest-grossing tour of the year.

- Swift buys a beachside mansion in Watch Hill, Rhode Island, for $17.75 million.

- Swift wins eight BBMAs, including the prize for Top Artist.

- David Mueller, a Denver-based DJ, allegedly gropes Swift's bottom while they pose together for a photo at a meet-and-greet before a concert. Swift tells her team what happened after Mueller and the fans leave the room, and her security removes him from the concert. KYGO, his employer, later fires Mueller after conducting an investigation into the incident.

- Swift wins the VMA for Best Female Video for "I Knew You Were Trouble."

- The Country Music Hall of Fame and Museum opens the Taylor Swift Education Center, funded by a $4 million donation from the singer, in Nashville. The center provides hands-on music education opportunities and exhibits for young people.

- Swift becomes the second artist (after Garth Brooks) to receive the Pinnacle Award at the CMA Awards. The award, which is not given every year, recognizes an artist who has reached a unique level of success in country music.

- Swift wins Favorite Female Artist—Pop/Rock, Favorite Female Artist—Country, Favorite Country Album (for *Red*), and Artist of the Year at the AMAs.

2014

- Swift moves to New York City, purchasing an apartment that had previously belonged to Peter Jackson.

- Swift gets her second cat, a Scottish fold named for Detective Olivia Benson of *Law & Order: SVU*.

- Swift has a small role in the film *The Giver*, starring alongside Jeff Bridges and Meryl Streep.

- Swift releases the single "Shake It Off," which becomes her second *Billboard* Hot 100 number one single. It is the lead single from *1989*.

- Swift is named *Billboard* Woman of the Year, becoming the first artist to earn the honor twice.

- *1989*, Swift's first pure pop album, is released. The album is named after Swift's birth year and is meant to represent a rebirth for the singer and her sound. It was also inspired by the synth-pop music, bright sounds and colors, and sense of independence of the 1980s. She worked again with Martin and Shellback and brought on new producers Jack Antonoff and Ryan Tedder to make the album. When she decided to make a pop album Swift faced pushback from her label, who feared leaving behind her country music roots altogether, but she persisted to make the record she envisioned. "Welcome to New York," "Bad Blood," and "Blank Space" are a few of the pop singles released from the album. *1989* debuts at number one on the *Billboard* 200 chart and sells 1.287 million copies in the first week, far exceeding most media predictions.

- On the same day that *1989* is released, New York City names Swift its Global Welcome Ambassador.

- Swift announces that she will donate all proceeds from the sale of the single "Welcome to New York" to New York City public schools.

- Swift pulls her back catalog from Spotify several months after arguing in a *Wall Street Journal* op-ed that music on streaming services should not be available for free. *1989* never had an initial release on Spotify.

- Swift wins the inaugural Dick Clark Award for Excellence at the AMAs, honoring the fact that she is the only artist to have sold 1 million copies of three different albums within the first week of their respective releases.

- The Grammy Museum presents the exhibit *The Taylor Swift Experience*, featuring handwritten lyrics, photographs, tour paraphernalia, and other artifacts from the singer's career.

- Swift is included in the "Barbara Walters Presents: The 10 Most Fascinating People of 2014" TV special.

2015

- Swift wins the Brit Award for International Female Solo Artist.

- Swift begins dating DJ and producer Calvin Harris.

- Swift reveals on Tumblr that her mother, Andrea, has been diagnosed with cancer. She encourages her fans to get screened for cancer and to urge their loved ones to get screened as well.

- Swift is presented with the 50th Anniversary Milestone Award at the 50th Annual ACM Awards. Andrea Swift presents Taylor with the award.

- The *1989* World Tour kicks off in Tokyo, Japan. Surprise guests ranging from Mick Jagger to Ellen DeGeneres come out onstage at each show. The tour goes on to earn over $250 million in revenue, surpassing her previous three solo tours.

- Swift wins eight BBMAs (including awards for Top Artist and Top Female Artist), becoming the most decorated artist in the history of the awards show. She also premieres the music video for "Bad Blood" at the ceremony.

- *Forbes* lists Swift 64th on its list of the World's 100 Most Powerful Women.

- Swift writes an open letter to Apple Music decrying the fact that the service would not be paying artists for the streams they received during the service's free three-month trial period. In less than a week, Apple Music changes its policy and announces that it will pay artists during the three-month trial. In turn, Swift announces that she will release *1989* (as well as the rest of her albums) on Apple Music.

- David Mueller, the Denver DJ accused of groping Swift, sues her for slander, saying she took away his career opportunities on the basis of a false charge. Mueller also claims that his former boss at KYGO radio station, Eddie Haskell, was the one who actually groped Swift. In October, a month after Mueller files his lawsuit, Swift countersues. The suit states that Swift is well aware of who groped her and demands that the case be tried before a jury. Her countersuit asks for $1 in damages.

- Swift wins the Emmy for Outstanding Creative Achievement in Interactive Media—Original Interactive Program for "AMEX Unstaged: The Taylor Swift Experience," a video that allows fans to explore the setting of the "Blank Space" music video.

- Songwriter Jessie Braham files a suit accusing Swift of plagiarizing his song "Haters Gone Hate" in "Shake It Off." The judge memorably references some of Swift's own lyrics in her dismissal of the lawsuit.

- Swift wins Adult Contemporary Artist, Favorite Album—Pop/Rock (for *1989*), and Song of the Year (for "Bad Blood") at the AMAs.

- Swift releases *The* 1989 *World Tour Live* concert special on Apple Music as one of the service's first big video releases.

2016

- Swift wins Best Music Video (for "Bad Blood"), Best Pop Vocal Album, and Album of the Year (both for *1989*) at the 58th Annual Grammy Awards. She becomes the first woman to win Album of the Year twice. (Her first win was for *Fearless*.) In her speech, she encourages women to ignore the voices that undercut their success.

- Swift donates $250,000 to help with Kesha's legal expenses after Kesha's injunction to break her contract with producer Dr. Luke's Sony imprint is denied in court.

- Swift wins the first-ever Taylor Swift Award at the 64th Annual BMI Pop Awards.

- Swift wins a BBMA for Top Touring Artist.

- Swift wins the Guinness World Record for Highest Annual Earnings Ever for a Female Pop Star.

- Swift dates actor Tom Hiddleston.

- Calvin Harris, Swift's former boyfriend, responds on Twitter to rumors that Swift helped write his song "This Is What You Came For" under the pen name Nils Sjoberg. Harris confirms the rumor and congratulates Swift on the quality of her songwriting but accuses her of trying to bury him like she buried Katy Perry (with whom she also reportedly had an ongoing feud). Harris and Swift had evidently agreed to keep her authorship a secret so their relationship wouldn't overshadow the song.

- *Forbes* names Swift the year's top-earning celebrity. She earns $170 million in 2016.

- David Mueller attempts to have Swift's groping counter-suit thrown out of court, but his request is denied.

- Swift writes the song "Better Man" for country group Little Big Town. The group initially keeps her contribution a secret, stating that they did not want her name to distract from the song itself.

2017

- Swift starts dating actor Joe Alwyn. Swift successfully keeps her relationship with Alwyn secret for several months, and to maintain their privacy the two do not make red carpet appearances together or discuss their relationship in interviews.

- Swift's back catalog is put on Spotify. *1989* had never been released on the streaming service. Big Machine Label Group states that the albums were put back on Spotify to celebrate the fact that *1989* sold 10 million copies. Some speculate that the June 9 date was chosen because it is the day Katy Perry's album *Witness* is released.

- Swift and Mueller appear in a civil court case in Denver, Colorado. After a trying four-day period of testimony from Swift and her team, including her mother, Andrea, the eight-person jury rules in favor of Swift, saying that Swift was assaulted by Mueller and that her team did not illegally seek his termination. Swift is awarded $1 in damages.

- Swift makes a donation to the Joyful Heart Foundation, which helps survivors of sexual assault.

- Swift wipes her social media accounts, igniting speculation that a new album is coming. Soon after clearing the accounts, she posts videos of a snake, teasing the themes and imagery of *Reputation*.

- "Look What You Made Me Do" is released. It is streamed 8 million times within a day of its release, breaking the previous record for first-day streams. The song and accompanying music video address the controversy and media speculation that had engulfed Swift over the previous few years, referencing her feuds with Kanye West, Katy Perry, and Calvin Harris and satirizing the over-the-top portrayals of her made in the media.

- *Reputation* is released. The album leans into Swift's new backstabbing, snakelike persona before pivoting to a set of delicate love songs reportedly inspired by Swift's boyfriend Joe Alwyn. She brought on only Max Martin, Shellback, and Jack Antonoff as producers, all of whom by this time were trusted collaborators. "... Ready for It," "Gorgeous," and "Delicate" are also released as singles from the album, in addition to "Look What You Made Me Do." Swift doesn't do any interviews or media appearances around the release, although she does partner with UPS, Target, and AT&T to promote the album. It goes to number one on the *Billboard* 200 chart and sells more than 1.2 million copies in its first week.

- Swift is named a *Time* Person of the Year as one of the #MeToo movement's "Silence Breakers." In the article she is interviewed about her sexual assault and the ensuing civil court case, and she encourages survivors of sexual assault not to blame themselves for their experiences.

2018

- Swift announces on Instagram that she has made a donation to March for Our Lives, a movement that advocates for gun reform.

- Swift returns to The Bluebird Cafe for a surprise performance with songwriter Craig Wiseman. She performs "Shake It Off," "Love Story," and "Better Man," a song she had originally written for Little Big Town.

- The *Reputation* Stadium Tour gets started in Glendale, Arizona, and continues to North America, Europe, Oceania, and Asia. The tour breaks the record for the highest-grossing North American tour by a female artist.

- At one of her first awards show appearances after an extended hiatus, Swift wins BBMAs for Top Female Artist and Top Selling Album.

- For the first time, Swift explicitly states her political views and endorses candidates running for office. In an Instagram post, she voices her support for Phil Bredesen and Jim Cooper, both running in the midterm elections in Tennessee and both Democratic candidates. In her post she also advocates for rights for women, LGBTQ people, and people of color. Vote.org reports that about 166,000 new voters, nearly half of whom are between ages eighteen and twenty-nine, register to vote on the site in the first twenty-four hours after Swift's political announcement.

- Swift wins AMAs for Artist of the Year, Favorite Female Artist—Pop/Rock, Favorite Album—Pop/Rock, and Tour of the Year. With these awards, she also becomes the most-awarded female artist in the history of the AMAs.

- Swift signs a multialbum contract with Universal Music Group. The agreement allows Swift to own all of her future master recordings. The label group also agrees to distribute the money from the sale of its Spotify shares back to its artists on a "non-recoupable" basis. This means that, even if artists have not made back all the money on Universal's advances to them, they will receive cash from Spotify sales.

2019

- Swift wins Tour of the Year and Best Music Video (for "Delicate") at the iHeartRadio Music Awards. In her speech, she thanks her fans for making the *Reputation* Stadium Tour a success when so many people thought it would flop. She also tells fans that when there is new music, they'll be the first to know.

- Swift donates $113,000 to the Tennessee Equality Project, a group that lobbies for the rights of LGBTQ people in the state of Tennessee.

- Swift is included in *Time*'s 100 Most Influential People list. Pop singer Shawn Mendes writes the accompanying essay about her.

- Swift commissions a new mural of a butterfly in Nashville. Created by artist Kelsey Montague, the butterfly's wings are filled with hearts, cats, rainbows, and flowers.

- After weeks of teasing on social media, Swift releases the single "ME!" The upbeat pop song is an ode to self-love, and its candy-colored music video is chock-full of small details, including photos of "cool chicks" (including members of the musical group The Chicks), a snake that explodes into pink butterflies, and Swift's new kitten, Benjamin Button.

- Following clues she left in the "ME!" music video, Swift goes on Instagram live to announce her upcoming album, *Lover*. That night, she releases the second single from the album, "You Need to Calm Down."

- Scott Borchetta, founder of Swift's former record label, Big Machine Records, sells the masters for her first six albums to Scooter Braun. Swift attempts to buy them herself but chooses not to when the deal includes a contract requiring her to record six new albums for the label to "earn back" the old ones. Swift considers Braun to be a "manipulative" bully and does not want him profiting off of her music. She turns down a further opportunity to buy her masters back from Braun when the deal requires signing an NDA that would only allow her to speak positively about him. In an interview with CBS News Sunday Morning, Swift announces that she will rerecord all of her albums so that she can own her own masters, devaluing Braun's versions.

- *Lover*, her seventh studio album, is released. *Lover* is the first album Swift releases under her new contract with Universal Music Group label Republic Records, which allows her to own the masters. The album is bright and upbeat, mostly consisting of love songs attributed to her relationship with Joe Alwyn. She also uses the era to showcase her support for LGBTQ+ rights, especially in the song and music video "You Need To Calm Down." In contrast to *Reputation*, Swift promotes the album through social media, interviews, talk shows, and other televised events. She releases singles "Me!", "You Need to Calm Down," "The Archer," and "The Man."

- Swift announces dates for her 2020 tour Lover Fest, intended to be a short tour consisting of festival-style shows in several European and South American cities as well as Los Angeles and Boston.

- Swift wins Artist of the Decade, Artist of the Year, Favorite Pop/Rock Female Artist, Favorite Adult Contemporary Artist, and Favorite Music Video for "You Need to Calm Down" at the AMAs.

- Swift appears as Bombalurina in the film adaptation of *Cats*.

- *Lover* breaks the Guinness world record for Biggest-Selling Album Worldwide For A Solo Artist.

2020

- *Miss Americana* is released on Netflix. The documentary charts the making of the *Lover* album, Swift's songwriting process, and her challenges with fame as well as finding peace in a more private life. The documentary also discusses her political stance more openly, showing her conflict with her team as she decides to speak out in favor of Democratic candidates in the 2018 midterms.

- Swift postpones her Lover Fest tour because of the COVID-19 pandemic.

- Swift updates her Instagram grid to show a black-and-white photo of her standing in the woods, a stylistic change from her previous album eras. Later that day, she announces that the image is the cover to her surprise eighth studio album, *Folklore*, which will be released that midnight.

- *Folklore* becomes a pop culture phenomenon and the biggest selling album of 2020. The album showcases Swift's songwriting skills, featuring songs based on fictional and historical characters as well as her own life. The sound of the album leans more towards indie ballads than Swift's usual pop style. The mature lyrics combined with the new sound bring near-universal critical acclaim and an expanded audience for Swift's work. *Folklore* was written and recorded during the pandemic, working mostly remotely with Jack Antonoff and Aaron Dessner. The content of the album is inspired by Swift's imagination in isolation at the beginning of the pandemic.

- Swift announces the documentary *Folklore: The Long Pond Studio Sessions* and accompanying album, releasing them that midnight. The documentary, which streams on Disney+, shows Swift performing all of the songs from *Folklore* and discussing its creation with Aaron Dessner and Jack Antonoff. The film is the first that Swift directs and produces herself. The film and live album are both well-received.

- In December, Swift once again posts a set of photos that add up to a picture of her in a forest. That night, she drops *Evermore*, which she describes as a sister album to *Folklore*. Like *Folklore*, some of the songs were written in isolation, but Swift also recorded many of them with Dessner and Antonoff after filming their documentary at Long Pond Studios. *Evermore* is similar in style to *Folklore*, with stories drawn both from Swift's imagination and real life. While continuing the indie vibe of *Folklore*, *Evermore* is somewhat more experimental musically.

- Swift wins AMAs for Artist of the Year and Favorite Pop/ Rock Female Artist, as well as Favorite Music Video for "Cardigan."

2021

- Swift officially cancels Lover Fest, sending refunds to fans who had purchased tickets.

- Swift wins the Album of the Year Grammy for *Folklore*.

- *Fearless (Taylor's Version)*, Swift's first rerecorded album, is released. "Love Story (Taylor's Version)," the first of her rerecorded singles, reaches number one on *Billboard*'s Hot Country Songs Chart, making her the first artist since Dolly Parton to achieve a number one with both an original and rerecorded version of the same song. The album reaches the top of the charts, and reviews from fans and critics are generally positive, praising Swift's improved vocals and stronger instrumentation.

- *Red (Taylor's Version)*, Swift's second rerecorded album, is released. Swift promotes the album through several talk show appearances, a Starbucks partnership, and a performance on *Saturday Night Live*. The album includes twenty tracks from the original deluxe edition as well as six new tracks, three separately released tracks, and a ten-minute version of "All Too Well," a fan favorite original *Red* song. Swift also writes and directs a short film as a music video for the song, depicting the song's story of an autumn romance and heartbreak.

- Swift again wins Favorite Pop/Rock Female Artist at the AMAs, along with Favorite Pop/Rock album for *Evermore*.

- Swift wins Top *Billboard* 200 Artist and Top Female Artist at the *Billboard* Music Awards.

- Swift wins the Global Icon Award at the Brit Awards.

- *Folklore* wins a Grammy for Album of the Year.

2022

- Swift receives an honorary Doctor of Fine Arts from New York University and delivers a speech at the university's commencement ceremony.

- *Midnights*, Swift's tenth studio album, is released. *Midnights* marks a return to pop after the cottagecore folk influences in *Folklore* and *Evermore*. Swift describes *Midnights* as a concept album exploring sleepless nights from throughout her life. At three a.m. on release day, she releases *Midnights (3am Edition)*, including several songs that were cut from the main album. The album includes singles "Anti-Hero," "Lavender Haze," and "Karma." Although some fans brought in during the *Folklore* era are disappointed, critical reception for *Midnights* is overwhelmingly positive.

- Swift becomes the first ever artist to occupy the entire top ten in the Hot 100 in one week.

- Swift announces the Eras Tour, conceived as a journey through her entire career. During the presale alone, 2 million tickets, making up 90 percent of the seats available for her North American show, are sold; the general sale is canceled due to lack of inventory. The tour is incredibly successful, with cities noting that her shows positively impact the local economy wherever she performs.

- Swift announces that she will direct a feature film for Searchlight Pictures. The next week, she appears on *Variety*'s "Directors on Directors" interview opposite Martin McDonagh, discussing her process and her transition from creating music to directing music videos and her aspirations for film.

- Swift wins Best Long Form Video and Video of the Year for *All Too Well: The Short Film* at the VMAs.

- Swift wins Artist of the Year, Favorite Country Female Artist, and Favorite Pop/Rock Female Artist at the AMAs. She also wins Favorite Music Video for *All Too Well: The Short Film* and Favorite Country Album and Favorite Pop Album for *Red (Taylor's Version)*.

- Swift wins Top *Billboard* 200 Artist, Top Country Artist, and Top Country Female Artist at the BBMAs. *Fearless (Taylor's Version)* is nominated for Top Country Album, but *Red (Taylor's Version)* wins.

2023

- Swift wins the Best Music Video Grammy for *All Too Well: The Short Film*. The film also wins Best Short Film at the Hollywood Critics Association Film Awards.

- Swift wins Favorite Female Artist at the Nickelodeon Kids' Choice Awards. She also wins Favorite Album for *Midnights* and Favorite Pet for her cat, Olivia Benson.

- The Eras Tour begins in Glendale, Arizona, where the show generates more revenue for the city's businesses than the Super Bowl, which was held in the same stadium one month before.

- Swift wins the Innovator Award at the iHeartRadio Music Awards. She also wins Pop Album of the Year for *Midnights*, Song of the Year and Best Lyrics for "Anti-Hero," TikTok Bop of the Year for "Bejeweled," and Favorite Use of a Sample for "Question... ?."

- Swift breaks up with long-term partner Joe Alwyn. Around the time the news leaks, she releases "Hits Different" and "You're Losing Me," songs fans interpret as describing the end of the relationship.

- Swift wins Best Song for "Carolina" at the MTV Movie & TV Awards.

- Swift releases "Cruel Summer" as a single from *Lover*, nearly four years after the release of the album. The song had been climbing the charts as a fan favorite during the Eras tour, leading her label to take the unusual step of promoting such an old song.

- *Speak Now (Taylor's Version)* is released. The rerecorded album contains six new "From the Vault" songs, but like the original, all of them were written solely by Swift. Although some critics and fans consider that with Swift's more mature voice the album has lost some of its charm, it receives rave reviews.

- At the VMAs, Swift wins Video of the Year, Song of the Year, Best Pop, Best Direction, Best Cinematography, and Best Visual Effects for "Anti-Hero." *Midnights* wins Album of the Year. Swift also wins Artist of the Year and Show of the Summer.

- Swift begins dating Kansas City Chiefs tight end, Travis Kelce. Kelce's jersey sales increase by 400 percent the day of the first game she attends, and viewership among women increases by more than 2 million people at the second game she attends.

- Swift releases *Taylor Swift: The Eras Tour*, a film of the Eras tour show. It becomes the highest-grossing concert film of all time.

- Bloomberg declares Swift a billionaire based on the estimated value of her music, houses, streaming deals, concert tickets, and merchandise.

- *1989 (Taylor's Version)* is released October 27. The album achieves the biggest streaming day of 2023 on Spotify and of all time on Apple Music; it's also Swift's thirteenth *Billboard* 200 number-one album, and the highest vinyl sales week of the twenty-first century. Like her previous rerecorded albums, *1989 (Taylor's Version)* is critically acclaimed, especially for her improved vocals and new vault tracks.

- Swift is named *Time*'s Person of the Year in December.

2024

- Swift wins Album of the Year and Best Pop Vocal Album, both for *Midnights*, at the 66th Annual Grammy Awards. During her acceptance speech she announces her next album, *The Tortured Poets Department*, will be released on April 19. Swift admits she began creating it immediately after finishing *Midnights* and worked on it secretly during the Eras Tour.

Glossary

ATTRIBUTE	(verb): assign to
BANDWIDTH	(noun): the mental or emotional energy needed to do something
CATALYST	(noun): an event that starts a sequence of following events
CINEMATIC	(adj): like a movie
DEMOGRAPHIC	(noun): a specific section of the population identified by a common trait
DIARISTIC	(adj): in the style of a diary, personal
DISINGENU-OUS	(adj): dishonest or not sincere
DISPEL	(verb): get rid of
EMPATHETIC	(adj): able to understand and be sensitive to the feelings or thoughts of another person
ENAMORED	(adj): feeling love and affection toward
ENTOURAGE	(noun): group of people who surround someone and assist them with their needs
EPIPHANY	(noun): realization or discovery
EXHILARATING	(adj.): causing strong feelings of happiness and excitement
FABRICATED	(adj): made-up or invented
FATALISTIC	(adj): believing future events are fixed and humans can't change them
FLUCTUATIONS	(noun): changes and shifts

FORCE MAJEURE	(noun): a big, unavoidable, unforeseeable event
GIG	(noun): a small, live performance for a musician
GRACIOUS	(adj): kind and generous
GRAVITATE	(verb): to be drawn to a person, place, or idea
INANE	(adj): pointless and insignificant
INEXPLICABLE	(adj): impossible to explain
INNOVATION	(noun): the creation or invention of something new
INTIMIDATED	(adj): afraid of or threatened by
INTRINSICALLY	(adj): naturally, automatically
INVOKING	(verb): calling forth as explanation
JUXTAPOSE	(verb): place two things in contrast with one another
LEGACY	(noun): what someone leaves behind, what people remember of them
MINUTIAE	(noun): tiny details
NON-RECOUP-ABLE	(adj): not able to regain
NOSTALGIA	(noun): feeling of longingly looking back on a memory
PARLAY	(verb): to turn one thing into something else more desirable
PATERNITY TEST	(noun): a medical test that determines if a person is the father of a particular child
PERCEPTION	(noun): a way of understanding something
PERSISTENT	(adj): refusing to give up, set on something

PRESUMPTU-OUS	(adj): taking things for granted, making assumptions
PREVALENT	(adj): common or widespread
PROFOUND	(adj): deep or insightful
RATIONAL	(adj): reasonable or logical
RELEVANCE	(noun): importance to the matter at hand
REVELATION	(noun): realization
RIGOROUSLY	(adv): strictly, intensely
SCRUTINIZED	(verb): looked at very closely, analyzed
SEMBLANCE	(noun): appearance or resemblance
SPONTANEOUS	(adj): sudden, unexpected
TAXIDERMIST	(noun): a person who preserves dead animals by preparing and stuffing them, often in life-like poses, so the animals can be displayed or studied
TRAJECTORY	(noun): path
TRIVIALIZES	(verb): makes something seem unimportant or silly
UNSOLICITED	(adj): not asked for
VENUES	(noun): locations where events (performances, for example) take place
VINTAGE	(adj): aged or antique
VULNERABILITY	(noun): a quality of emotional openness that often reveals a person's fears or weaknesses
WORK ETHIC	(noun): set of beliefs around hard work and determination

Additional Resources

On Taylor Swift

Esquivel, Eric M. *Female Force: Taylor Swift*. Tidalwave, 2023.

- This biographical comic pays tribute to Swift's remarkable career, including her record-breaking Eras Tour. It's part of a series of comics that highlight female forces in music, pop culture, politics.

Folklore: The Long Pond Studio Sessions. Disney+, 2020.

- Swift directed and produced this documentary set in a remote recording studio in New York. She performs all of the tracks from *Folklore* and also discusses the creative process behind them.

Hunt, Helena (editor). *Taylor Swift: In Her Own Words*. Agate, 2019.

- This is the full-length title from which this Young Reader edition was created. The full-length version includes additional quotations from Taylor Swift.

Miss Americana. Netflix, 2020.

- This documentary about Swift dives into her professional and personal life during the period between *Reputation* and *Lover*, revealing intimate details and offering a raw, honest look into her life.

On Songwriting and the Music Business

Bell, Ed. *How to Write a Song (Even If You've Never Written One Before and You Think You Suck)*. The Song Foundry, 2020.

- A step-by-step guide for beginners to craft a song idea, lyrics, and music—and put them all together to make a great song.

Dylan, Bob. *The Philosophy of Modern Song*. Simon & Schuster, 2022.

- Bob Dylan examines some of the most iconic songs from recent decades and explores what makes them great.

Hollander, Sam. *21-Hit Wonder: Flopping My Way to the Top of the Charts*. Holt, 2022.

- Renowned songwriter Sam Hollander offers stories of his own flops as well as inspiration for artists who want to make it to the top of the charts.

Rakim. *Sweat the Technique: Revelations on Creativity from the Lyrical Genius*. Amistad, 2019.

- Part memoir, part writing guide—hip-hop legend Rakim shares his philosophy on words, writing, and rhyming.

Tweedy, Jeff. *How to Write One Song: Loving the Things We Create and How They Love Us Back*. Dutton, 2020.

- Wilco guitarist Jeff Tweedy breaks down the mystery and magic of songwriting into a manual for music, lyrics, and the joy of creation.

White, Emily. *How to Build a Sustainable Music Career and Collect All Revenue Streams*. Podcast audio, 2021–.

- Based on White's bestselling book of the same name, this podcast offers a methodical guide for building a long-term music career from recording to distributing to marketing and more.

On Women in the Music Industry

Bennet, Christine. *Musical Women Throughout History: The Women Who Fought for Music*. Flying Cat, 2022.
- Musical history tends to focus on the men. This collection unearths the pioneering women who were the musical geniuses of their time.

Keys, Alicia with Michelle Burford. *More Myself: A Journey*. Flatiron, 2020.
- Grammy-winning artist Alicia Keys shares her journey through the ups and downs of the music industry and fame.

Parton, Dolly and Robert K. Oermann. *Dolly Parton, Songteller: My Life in Lyrics*. Chronicle, 2020.
- The beloved icon tells the stories behind her famous lyrics.

Turner, Myra Faye. *The Untold Stories of Female Artists, Musicians, And Writers*. Atlantic, 2018.
- This collection of biographical stories explores the lives of history's lesser-known women in the arts and their boundary-breaking talents.

Acknowledgments

We would like to thank John Crema, Kelsey Dame, Amanda Gibson, Morgan Krehbiel, Emma Kupor, Erin Rosenberg, and Jameka Williams for their invaluable contributions to the preparation of this manuscript.